PETER LORD

BAKER BOOK HOUSE
Grand Rapids, Michigan 49516

ISBN: 0-8010-5650-0

Twenty-second printing, August 2001

Printed in the United States of America

For current information about all releases from
Baker Book House, visit our web site:
http://www.bakerbooks.com/

To

Johnnie

wife, friend, partner

who demonstrated daily for thirty years the truths in this book,

whose lifestyle can be explained only by an indwelling Christ,

whom I can describe only in this way: "one heaven of a woman."

Contents

Part 5: Fellowshiping with God Through Hearing His Voice

Love must express and communicate itself.
    That's its nature.
When people love one another, they start telling
    Everything that's happened to them,
Every detail of their daily life, they "Reveal" themselves
    To each other, unbosom themselves
    And exchange confidences.
God hasn't ceased being Revelation any more
    Than He's ceased being Love.
    He enjoys expressing Himself.
Since He's Love, He must give Himself,
Share His secrets, communicate with us
    And reveal Himself to anyone
        Who wants to Listen.[1]

1. Louis Eberly, *Alive Now!* (Nashville, Tenn.), a 64-page magazine published six times yearly by the United Methodist Church.

Introduction

W hat we have seen and heard," the apostle John says in his first letter, "we proclaim to you also, that you also may have fellowship with us; and indeed our fellowship is with the Father and with His Son Jesus Christ" (1 John 1:3).

I took John seriously. I believed he meant those words for all of us. I have had fellowship with the Father and His Son Jesus Christ. And, to paraphrase, these things I now write to *you* to let you know that 1 John 1:3 can be experienced in reality by anyone who is a child of God.

Our heavenly Father wants fellowship with us. He wants to commune and communicate with us in a true fellowship of love and enjoyment of each other. It is imperative to understand this as the focus and purpose of this book — *Hearing God.*

This book has not been written to help us "get more from God," but to enable us to have fellowship with him. And fellowship is impossible if we cannot hear him as well as talk with him. "God is faithful, through whom you were called into fellowship with His Son Jesus Christ, our Lord" (1 Cor. 1:9).

The Scriptures and Hearing God

Do the Scriptures teach us that we can and should hear God speak to us today? Is this a clear, important, repeated teaching — or is it one that can be supported only by manipulating small portions of Scripture to prove a point?

There has been so much damage done in the Christian world on the basis of "God said," that we must be cautious. If there is a strong basis in Scripture for us to hear God speak to us today, then we may appropriate and experience this by faith. If not, we ought to stay as far away as possible from this idea.

As we prepare to look at the evidence in Scripture for hearing God speak to us today — biblical instruction, promises, and commands — let us explore a few questions to stimulate our thinking:

1. What is more important — an author or the book he or she writes?
2. Who is better able to interpret and explain a book than its author?
3. What should we worship — the Bible or the God the Bible proclaims?
4. How can we find God's will for most things of life unless he tells us?
5. Why is it that so much division has been caused by the Bible — which teaches that Christians ought to be unified?
6. How did Christians from earlier centuries make it? What about the Christians who were born before Guttenberg invented the printing press — and therefore never owned a Bible? Like many Christians today, especially in Third World countries, they could not have read it anyway. So how did they manage to live the Christian life?

The Purpose of Scripture

I still have the love letters my wife wrote to me during our courtship days. Though I keep them because I treasure them, my focus is not on them, but on her. They told me of her love for me then, and I am still experiencing it now!

Suppose I had memorized those love letters. Or decoupaged them and put them all over my house. Or even wrote books on the wonder of her words. If I had never come to her, never had time for her, then I would have missed the whole purpose of the letters!

Similarly, the Scriptures are not an end in themselves. They point the way to a meaningful relationship with the living God. They bring us into fellowship with him as they demonstrate his love. Our response is to love him with everything we are and have — and to show that love in obedience. "You search the Scriptures, because you think that in them you have eternal life; and it is these that bear witness of Me; and you are unwilling to come to Me, that you may have life" (John 5:39–40).

The Scriptures are letters to us from God through special secretaries like Moses, prophets, apostles, and others — letters urging us to come to him for fellowship.

It is obvious that a photo is a picture of a person. It is not actually the person, but a reminder of the person and what he or she looks like. We keep pictures of people we love in our wallets and frame them for our homes and offices. We keep them in photo albums as representatives and reminders of people we care for. Though they are a substitute for those people in their absence, they are not enough to take the place of the people themselves.

In the same way, the Scriptures are a photo album of Jesus Christ. In Scripture we see him as he performs and acts out his role as Savior. We see him also as Teacher-Friend-Counselor-Healer-Helper and in many other roles according to our need.

But along with those word pictures are the Lord's current address and phone number. Jesus is saying to us, "Come to me so that I can be to you now what I was in the past to others." If we do not come, we have missed the primary purpose of the Scriptures.

Over and over and over again, Jesus taught the importance, the *necessity*, of hearing God speak to us. Jesus' most-repeated statement (fifteen times in the New Testament) was: "He that hath ears to hear, let him hear!" The last seven times he said it (in Revelation 2 and 3), Jesus added ". . . what the Spirit is saying" — because Jesus was speaking from heaven, where he had already returned, and the Holy Spirit was here on earth.

We know that Jesus defined his followers as "those who hear my voice, and I know them, and they follow me" (John 10). On one occasion, Jesus' mother and brothers could not get near him because of the crowd. So they sent him a message, saying they wished to see him. He turned their request into a vivid demonstration of the importance of hearing God by describing the members of his physical birth-family as those who "hear the word of God and do it" (Luke 8:21).

The Lord Jesus told us we are to live as he lived and to minister as he ministered. Then he explained *how* he lived and ministered by declaring that he did nothing on his own initiative: "For I did not speak on My own initiative, but the Father Himself who sent Me has given Me commandment, what to say, and what to speak" (John 12:49).

Jesus told Martha that only one thing was necessary. It was what Mary was already doing: listening to his words. And he would not stop her! (Luke 10:41–42).

A Major New Testament Teaching

One of the strongest teachings of the New Testament is that God the Holy Spirit lives in the believer now, to be to the believer all that Jesus was to the disciples. This was one of Jesus' greatest promises.

That God lives in the believer was the promise Jesus made to the disciples saddened by the announcement of his imminent departure. "I will ask the Father," he declared, "and He will give you another Helper, that He may be with you forever" (John 14:16).

Then he explained further: the Helper "is the Spirit of truth, whom the world cannot receive, because it does not behold Him or know Him, but you know Him because He abides with you and will be in you. I will not leave you as orphans" (John 14:17–18a).

Later, in the same message to his disciples, Jesus made an even stronger statement: "I tell you the truth," Jesus said. "It is to your advantage that I go away; for if I do not go away, the Helper shall not come to you; but if I go, I will send Him to you" (John 16:7). One of the functions of the Holy Spirit, Jesus explained, would be to teach them all they needed to know — what Jesus had not been able to teach because they were not ready for it (vv. 12–13).

It is the teaching of the New Testament writers that the Christian norm is to walk in the Spirit. Paul, when he wrote to the Romans, specifically defined the children of God: those "who are being led by the Spirit of God" (Rom. 8:14).

"You abide in Jesus," John writes to believers and goes on to explain: "The anointing you received from Him [the Holy Spirit] abides in you, and you have no need for any one to teach you; but as His anointing teaches you about all things, and is true and is not a lie, and just as it has taught you, you abide in Him" (1 John 2:27).

There are so many other places in the New Testament teaching that God speaks to us that it would be impossible to list them all here. All of us who read Scripture as God's Word will hear his voice clearly.

Experiencing the Promises of Scripture

There is no way we can experience many of the promises of Scripture unless we know God and hear him speaking to us. Take, for example, that verse in James we all love to quote and to claim: "If any of you lacks wisdom, let him ask of God, who gives to all men generously and without reproach, and *it will be given to him*" (James 1:5 [emphasis mine]).

How can we experience this if God does not tell us? If we do not hear from him?

When you and I pray as the Lord taught us in Matthew 6:10 — "Thy will be done on earth as it is in heaven"—are they just meaningless words to us? How can we know what his will is and do it if he does not tell us?

Most of the everyday decisions you and I have to make are not specifically covered in the Bible. Whom should you marry? What kind of vacation should you take? When and where should you take it? Should you buy this house? Is this the job the Lord wants you to take?

We struggle with such questions and agonize over our decisions. But the way to get the answers from God is clearly written for us.

Perhaps the greatest promise of all to the believer is the one Jesus made to us before he returned to the Father — the privilege of knowing God and having a personal and intimate experience with him (John 16:7, 12–13). This is impossible if we cannot hear him.

Dare we accuse him who so loved us of giving us stones when we long for bread? Why did the Lord promise the Holy Spirit, and why should the Holy Spirit come to live in us, if all we need are the Scriptures?

The Scriptures are only objective revelations as the Holy Spirit makes them so. Scripture and man without the Holy Spirit become a subjective revelation. That is, they mean what each individual thinks they mean. A look at all the contradictory ideas that different

Christians hold, all using the same Bible and even the same passage of Scripture, is enough to convince us that we need the Spirit of God to illuminate the truth.

In outlining the coming of the Holy Spirit, Jesus said he would live in us for many reasons. Among these — and possibly one of the most important — is that the Holy Spirit will guide us into all truth (John 16:13). He will take the Scriptures and tell us what they mean: what they mean for us *individually* and what they mean for us *now*.

To read and study the Scripture while ignoring its Author is one of the ways we "grieve" and quench the Holy Spirit (cf. Eph. 4:30). To grieve and quench the Holy Spirit is to grieve and quench Jesus Christ.

Listen to A. W. Tozer:

> The Bible will never be a living Book to us until we are convinced that God is articulate in His universe. To jump from a dead, impersonal world to a dogmatic Bible is too much for most people. They may admit that they *should* accept the Bible as the Word of God, and they may try to think of it as such, but they find it impossible to believe that the words there on the page are actually for them. A man may *say*, "These words are addressed to me," and yet in his heart not feel and know that they are. He is the victim of a divided psychology. He tries to think of God as mute everywhere else and vocal only in a book.
>
> I believe that much of our religious unbelief is due to a wrong conception of and a wrong feeling for the Scriptures of Truth. A silent God suddenly begins to speak in a book and when the book was finished lapsed back into silence again forever. . . .
>
> I think a new world will arise out of the religious mists when we approach our Bible with the idea that it is not only a book which was once spoken, but a book which is *now speaking*. The prophets habitually said, "Thus *saith* the Lord." They meant their hearers to understand that God's speaking is in the continuous present.[2]

Dangers of the Scripture Without the Author

Scripture itself speaks of the danger of reading it without the Author, warning us that "the letter kills, but the Spirit gives life" (2 Cor. 3:6).

2. A. W. Tozer, *The Pursuit of God* (Harrisburg, Penn.: Christian Publications, Inc., 1982), pp. 80–82.

Jesus' prayer at the end of his earthly ministry included a plea for unity in his disciples (John 17:23). And yet *God's written Word*, the Bible, has become the basis for division and animosities. Every denomination and even many individuals within denominations differ on what the Bible means. They use these differences of opinion as an excuse to withdraw, to criticize, and to condemn others.

Without the Author — the Holy Spirit — to interpret it for us, the Bible becomes a dividing wall, killing people's fellowship with one another. But when the Bible is read under the guidance of its Author, its words live and unify the church.

As previously mentioned, Jesus warned the people of the danger of reading the Scriptures and missing God. "You search the Scriptures," he said, "because you think that in them you have eternal life; and it is these that bear witness of Me; you are unwilling to come to Me, that you may have life" (John 5:39–40).

We know that the Scriptures were written to tell men about God. And we are amazed that so many people had read the Old Testament in such a distorted way that they missed God himself when he was standing right in front of them! There is still the danger today that Scripture — if not handled rightly — can keep us from the living God and a real relationship with him.

Scripture not only reveals God himself but also records his relationship to man in the past. It shows how God interacted with people. It tells what he did and why he did it and explains why people succeeded and why they failed. We learn through the Bible how others experienced the power, provision, protection, or punishment of God.

The Bible also contains prospects for the future. It tells what the future will be if we walk with God — and if we don't walk with him.

What we often fail to consider is that both the records of the past and the promises for the future are for motivation in the present. They are to demonstrate how you and I can experience God *now* and *here* in our own situation and life. What the Bible tells about God and his desire for man can be experienced right now.

The challenge to us is to take the Bible seriously. To personally experience the God it proclaims. To know, in the reality of daily living, his protection, provision, guidance, and all his other functions *now*. To be able to sing in truth, "You ask me how I know He lives? He lives within my heart."[3]

3. Alfred H. Ackley, "He Lives". Copyright 1933, 1961. The Rodeheaver Co., owner.

Inspired by the record of the past, encouraged by the promises of the future, let us live and walk with him *now* — "For in him we live and move and have our being . . ." (Acts 17:28, NIV).

Why I Started Listening to God

Into my life have come a series of unrelated events that all added up to motivation to experience the reality of hearing God's voice. (These events are not given in any sequence or order of importance.)

Skiing

While skiing in Colorado, I noticed on the slopes some people wearing red vests. On getting closer, I was able to read the words on them: BLIND SKIER.

This both gripped and puzzled me. I had a hard enough time skiing with two good eyes — and here were people with no eyesight skiing successfully. How did they do it? I had to find out!

The answer was that each one had a guide whose instructions the skier trusted totally, a guide who gave simple, specific instructions and directions.

The guide skied beside, behind, or in front of the blind person — but always in a place where they could communicate with each other. I found out that there were two basic forms of communication the guide used: the tapping together of ski poles to assure the blind person that the guide was there; and the speaking of simple instructions about what to do next. "Go right. Turn left. Stop. Slow. Skier coming up on your right." The only responsibility of the blind skier was to exhibit complete trust and immediate obedience to instructions.

Life is much like skiing downhill blind. We cannot see even five seconds into the future. We cannot see the struggles and tears to come — or all the other "skiers" who might run into us or we into them.

But God has given us the Holy Spirit to be our Guide through life. To walk with us and talk with us. Our only responsibility is to listen and obey. Before we can obey, we must listen. To listen, we need to know the voice of our Guide.

As I considered this, I wondered whether I could possibly hear God on a far greater basis than I had experienced thus far.

The Most-Asked Question

In thirty-six years of ministry, the question I get asked more than any other is: "How do you know God's voice? How can one know whether the thoughts are God's or from the devil?"

This was a question I could never answer fully — because I myself sometimes had the same question. It is a question that, by God's grace, I am now learning to answer for myself and those others who are really wanting to know.

"One Heaven of a Woman"

The only way I know to describe my wife is "one heaven of a woman." But this was not always the case!

Before our fourth anniversary, Johnnie had a nervous breakdown. It was caused by her determination, as a very sincere Christian, to be a godly person, mother, and wife at any cost. She carried the burden of trying to follow all she heard from good Christian leaders. It was too much.

While she was still undergoing shock treatments and medication, Johnnie heard one sentence a preacher said: "When Christ came to live in you, *all of him* came to live in you."

Her first response was, "I don't believe that." Johnnie knew that if the preacher's statement was true, she had no excuse for her present condition.

So she began to experiment, first in one situation, then in another. She discovered that Jesus *was* there, living in her — all of him — available to be all she needed at all times and in every situation.

I have watched her for thirty-two years now — and have never seen her blow a situation badly. Johnnie has learned to listen to the Indweller. He helps her and advises her and she is victorious. I watch her minister under his guidance and power and see amazing results.

My wife is just an "average" woman. Everyone who knows her agrees about that. But Johnnie is a winner because she has one important secret. Like Mary of Bethany, Johnnie knows how to listen to Jesus and follow him.

Modern-Day Prophets

Men whom God was obviously using — men whom I respected in the ministry — urged me: "God's voice must speak from within to bring enlightenment. It must be the Spirit of God speaking soundlessly within. That is what brings in man and makes him accountable to God."

A. W. Tozer recalls:

> Many years ago, the godly Horatius Bonar wrote: "A seared conscience is the sinner's heritage. It is upon this that the Holy Spirit first lays his hand when he awakens the soul from its sleep of death. He touches the conscience, and then the struggles of conviction come. He then pacifies it by the sprinkling of the blood, showing it Jesus and His cross. Then giving it the taste of forgiveness, it rests from all its tumults and fears."[4]

"Just the words of a Scripture text falling upon a human ear may not mean anything," says Tozer, but he adds:

> I believe that God has related these somehow: the voice of conviction in the conscience and the Holy Spirit, the point of contact, witnessing within man's being. A person has not been illuminated until that voice begins to sound within him.
>
> Men and women need to be told that it may be fatal to silence the inner voice. It is always perilous to resist the conscience within; but it may be fatal to silence that voice, to continue to ignore that speaking voice within![5]

God the Father

Another thing that motivated me to try to develop a hearing ear for God's voice was the realization that God is a father and is interested in being *my* Father.

4. A. W. Tozer, *Echoes from Eden* (Harrisburg, Penn.: Christian Publications, Inc., 1981), p. 62.

5. Ibid., pp. 62–63.

My early concept of God and his Son Jesus Christ is best illustrated by the word *boss*, someone for whom I worked. In an effort to please him, my response was work — hard work — and more work. I wanted so much to please God by my works that I was neglecting important aspects of my life and responsibility, such as my family. And, as a pastor, I not only worked but also got others to work, work, work, as another way of pleasing him.

Where did I get as my primary concept of God that he was The Boss? Not from him, but from others, especially from my religious peer group.

What a relief when, in the early seventies, my particular part of the church put an emphasis on God the Teacher! We changed from working to studying. Revival meetings were changed to bible conferences, using books and tapes and discussions on every conceivable subject. We sought more and more knowledge — and we got more and more of the disagreements that inevitably come from the knowledge that puffeth up.

Then I made the most important fundamental discovery about God: I found his real heart. As I began to listen in fellowship with him, I found out that God is first and foremost the Father!

Like any good parent, he is also Boss and Teacher. But first and above all else, he is the Father — *my* Father.

After this heart-shaking discovery, a series of personal events occurred. They included every area of my life — family, relationships, work, ministry. God spoke to me through them, and I experienced firsthand the ability to hear him. To know his wisdom, love, care, and strength. I will be sharing these experiences throughout this book.

There have been little and big life experiences for me, spiritual and material happenings that reflect God-given releases and restraints. Together they have convinced me in an ever-increasing way that I can experience daily — and in all areas of life — the fact that I have a heavenly Father who loves, cares, and knows me personally.

God, my Father "walks with me and talks with me."[6]

6. C. Austin Miles, "In the Garden." Copyright 1912 by Hall-Mack Co. Copyright renewal 1940 (extended). The Rodeheaver Co., owner. All rights reserved.

1

Checking Your Equipment

The computer
makes us fantastically more able
to calculate and analyze.

It does not help us to meditate.

We have instruments
to enable us to see everything
from the nebulae to the neutron —
    everything
except ourselves.

We have immeasurably extended
our gift of sight
but not of insight.

For that, we have the same equipment
as the eighth-century prophets.

Potentially the same,
    but actually poorer,
for while we have been so busy
extending one aspect of the knowing
    of telling self,
we have allowed other aspects to atrophy.

We have built ourselves up
into power transmitting stations,
but as receiving sets
we are feeble.[1]

1. John V. Taylor, *The Go-Between God* (New York: Oxford, 1979).

1

A Hearing Ear

During a wedding reception at our home some years ago, I stepped outside for a moment to escape the crowd and the noise. There, on the small path leading from the front door to the driveway, was one of the ushers. Head cocked, he was peering intently at the plantings beside the walk.

"What's up?" I half-whispered, trying to see what he was looking at and wondering what new escapade was being planned for the bride and groom.

"Mr. Lord," came the awed answer, "do you know that you have eighteen different kinds of crickets in those bushes?"

Crickets? I stared at him blankly. I had lived here for years and had never consciously heard a cricket!

But *he*, a graduate student in entomology at the University of Florida, had learned to distinguish over two hundred different types of cricket calls with his natural ear. Imagine learning to listen to crickets!

I suddenly understood that a person "learns" to hear and that a hearing ear can be developed. I also realized that there were many sounds I was not hearing.

> I was asleep,
>   but my heart was awake.
> A voice!
> My beloved was knocking:
> Open to me (Song of Sol. 5:2).

What a challenge to learn to listen to God! And because some of the secrets of listening to crickets can be related to our ability to hear God, I will share them with you.

A Basic Premise and a Choice

"He that hath ears to hear, let him hear."[2]

Fifteen times this statement made by our Lord is quoted in the New Testament. It indicates the importance of two things:

1. A basic premise: having ears to hear
2. A basic choice: choosing to use those ears to hear.

When one receives spiritual life at the new birth, one receives the abilities inherent in that spiritual life. God's gift of spiritual life contains the ability to hear *in* and *from* the spiritual world: "ears to hear." Without this ability, communion, meditation, and hearing our heavenly Father are not possible.

A baby is born with an inherent physical ability to hear but does not know what he hears. Likewise, a baby sees but knows not what he sees. *Understanding* — comprehension — must be learned.

Listening is the communication skill we practice most often, but many of us never really learn how to do it right. Communication experts consider careful listening to be a learned ability, not innate behavior.

According to Dr. Kyman K. Steil, chairman of the Speech-Communication Division, Department of Rhetoric, University of Minnesota at St. Paul, "We spend 80 per cent of our waking time communicating yet listening is the one communication skill we're never really taught."[3]

Sperry Corporation hired Dr. Steil to create a series of "seminars in listening" for its employees. Sperry now says of itself, "We understand how important it is to listen, because mistakes in listening can be expensive."

In the business world, companies have learned by trial and error the importance of learning to listen. In the spiritual realm, Chris-

2. Cf. Matt. 11:15; 13:9, 43; Mark 4:9, 23; 7:16; Luke 8:8; 14:35, etc.
3. Dr. Kyman K. Steil, quoted in USAir: September 1981.

tians equipped with "ears to hear" must learn to communicate with their Lord and Father in heaven in an ever-increasing way.

This is where *choice* comes in: choosing to use your ears to hear:

**If the capacity is there,
the ability must be developed.**

First Secret: Hearing God Must Be Vital to You

Something is "vital" if it is perceived as necessary to live the quality of life we choose to live. Using that definition, the best overall preparation for successful meditation involves a personal conviction of its importance and a staunch determination to persevere in its practice.

Jamaica, where I was born and reared, was once a British colony and used the British monetary system of pounds, shillings, and pence. After Jamaica received its independence, the system was changed to dollars and cents. The new government faced an immediate dilemma, however, because a good percentage of the population was illiterate.

Officials wondered, "How are the people going to learn to change from the pound to the dollar system? Must we hold classes to teach them?"

A wise man answered astutely, "It won't be necessary to have formal classes. Money is *vital* to the people. So they will learn the new system quickly and learn it correctly." And so they did.

The principle he expressed is true. People quickly learn what they consider vital to their lives.

In the case of my entomology friend, hearing crickets was vital to his goal of getting a doctorate from the university. He had ruled them into his life. Hearing crickets means nothing to me, so I had ruled them out as not being important.

If meditation is important to you, and you are staunchly determined to persevere in its practice whatever the cost, you are on the road to success. With this attitude of mind, you have made a splendid preparation for meditation.

In *Search for Silence*, Elizabeth O'Connor reminds us of St. Teresa's admonition: "It is essential, I maintain, to begin the practice of prayer with a firm resolution to persevere in it."[4] If you begin prayer

4. St. Teresa, *Way of Perfection*, xxi.

with the attitude that it is an absolute necessity, vital to sustain fellowship with Jesus, then you can be sure to make progress.

Author O'Connor continues:

> If one be not convinced of the necessity of meditation in his own life, nor resolved never to omit its daily exercise, he will soon give it up on one pretext or another. Therefore, one should not adopt the practice of meditation with the intention of "giving it a try"; but rather, one must undertake the exercise with a firm belief that it is of the utmost importance that he begin and persevere in it. Our mental attitude towards any enterprise will determine, to a large extent, our success in it; meditation is no exception.[5]

Why is it that people encounter God in a time of great need, or personal crisis, more than any other time?

The answer is very simple. Crises are situations we don't know how to handle, but which must be solved for our survival. Therefore, in a crisis we turn to God.

> **Our desperation —**
> **coupled with our inability,**
> **our weakness, our need —**
> **makes hearing from him**
> **an absolute necessity.**

The great tragedy is that most of us only come to God in crises. We move from crisis to crisis and never learn that we need him and his words for every part of life.

Until hearing God becomes *vital* to you and me, we are not likely to learn to hear either quickly or correctly.

The Scriptural Emphasis on Hearing

There was an air of excitement in the well-ordered home in Bethany. The Master had come. Mary was sitting at his feet, listening to their guest. Martha bustled around in the kitchen, making preparations for a meal.

Martha appealed to Jesus, asking that he tell Mary to help in the

5. Elizabeth O'Connor, *Search for Silence* (Waco, Tex.: Word Books, 1972), p. 141.

many preparations, but the Lord answered and said to her, "Martha, Martha! You are getting worried and upset about too many things. Only one thing is important. Mary has chosen the right thing, and it will never be taken away from her" (Luke 10:41–42).

Mary was the only one who really understood what was ahead for Jesus, because she had sat at his feet, listening to his words. Later, while the apostle Peter attempted to persuade the Lord not to go to his death, Mary anointed Jesus with oil in preparation for his death and burial.

A casual reading of the Bible by an unbiased mind would leave no doubt of the possibility — yes, the absolute necessity — of hearing God's voice. But the Bible gets down to specifics, too. Paul ties faith and hearing together, saying that "faith comes from hearing, and hearing by the word of Christ" (Rom. 10:17).

"Without faith," the writer to Hebrews was inspired to say, "no one can please God. Anyone who comes to God must believe that He is real and that He rewards those who truly want to find Him" (Heb. 11:6).

Jesus tells us that our direction, our goals, our very lives, must be built on his words to us: "Man shall not live on bread alone, but on every word that proceeds out of the mouth of God" (Matt. 4:4).

Elsewhere, Jesus gives us the secret of his own life, saying, "My food is to do the will of Him who sent Me, and to accomplish His work" (John 4:34). "The Son can do nothing of Himself, unless it is something He sees the Father doing; for whatever the Father does, these things the Son also does in like manner" (John 5:19).

Our Lord declared that he lived his whole life this way — his Father was the "programmer" of his life. He did the things placed in his mind by his Father.

This is the way God wants us to live our lives, too. If, as Jesus did, we would allow the Father to program our minds, we would walk in peace and power such as we have never known.

Johnnie and Prayer

My wife has learned to tune into God's voice. In growing-up situations with each of our children, Johnnie had to ask God to show her how to pray. He who is faithful answered — and Johnnie prayed according to the things God showed her.

Johnnie says, "It isn't *facts* that cause us to worry: it's our interpretation of the facts." Her story in *Learning How to Pray for Our Children* ends with this testimony:

> As mothers who believe in Him, we need to be assured that God *does* love that child, that He *does* have a plan, and that he *is working* whether we see it or not!
> We need to know that God loves that child even more than we as parents can. We need to know that God can be trusted to work in our child's life on His own schedule and in His own way to accomplish His purpose.[6]

In Jeremiah 29:11-12 the Lord in effect says: "I know what I have planned for you. I have good plans for you. I don't plan to hurt you. I plan to give you hope and a good future. Then you will call My name. You will come to Me and pray to Me. And I will listen to you."

Like Johnnie, people who have developed this kind of trust in God live in a great sense of peace, rest, and victory. They see his promises as reality. They understand and practice what it means to take "captive every thought to make it obedient to Christ" (2 Cor. 10:5).

This is living in God's presence and walking in his light. The enemy will do anything he can to prevent it — and the Lord Jesus does everything he can to aid us. But the choice really rests with us.

Developing a Hearing Ear

A key to hearing God's promises and acting as though they were already so is to command your mind, based on something God has said. You do this, says Marvin Moore, by

> . . . an act of the will, a decision only you can make, and which you must back up with all the mental and emotional strength you can muster. Pretend that your mind is a TV set, and when a program comes on that you have decided not to watch, flip the switch.[7]

6. Johnnie Lord, *Learning How to Pray for Our Children* (Titusville, Fla.: Agape Ministries, 1979), pp. 14–15.
7. Marvin Moore, *How to Handle Your Imagination* (Nashville, Tenn.: Southern Publishing Association, 1979), p. 45.

There are three steps to this process:

1. Make a deliberate choice and effort to set your mind on God. Ask his help if you think you have an undisciplined mind.
2. Make a deliberate choice to exercise your mind in focusing on God. The best way is to have a regular time to pursue this intensely. Like any other form of exercise, begin at a low level and increase gradually.
3. Carry this exercise of setting your mind on God into every area of life. Do it by determining to consciously bring every thought captive to God and immediately turning to God in all circumstances. After a while, it will become a spontaneous action to refer all things to him. It will become a natural reflex developed through habit.

In large letters an acrostic sign on the wall of a health spa read:

> **F — frequency**
> **I — intensity**
> **T — time**

That acronym for "FIT" is a principle for the development of any desired ability — in this case, hearing God. This principle is also essential for the maintenance of that capacity.

Paul tells us in Romans 8 that God's children are led by his Spirit, if that Spirit of God really lives in them. "But if anyone does not have the Spirit of Christ, he does not belong to Him" (v. 9). We *must* hear God if we are to live by the Spirit as sons of God (v. 14).

Hearing God is essential for a good Father/son relationship. Paul says, "Walk by the Spirit and you will not carry out the desire of the flesh" (Gal. 5:16).

> **The tap root of spiritual maturity is**
> **a personal,**
> **continuous,**
> **vital,**
> **loving**
> **relationship with Jesus Christ.**

Believers who truly understand scriptural concepts realize that hearing God is the one thing they cannot do without if they are going to live the Christian life.

Substitutes for Hearing from God

Satan's Tactics

Our churches are filled with spiritual babies who are failing to grow into the likeness of our Lord Jesus Christ. Despite all the supposed spiritual information and help accessible today, there is less spiritual health and slower-growing spiritual maturity than ever before.

The greatest hindrances to hearing God are all the substitutes, ready for immediate use. These may be helpful and even good in themselves on occasion. But, like many other things, when used as a *substitute* for the time, the effort, and the perseverance of hearing God for ourselves, they become problem areas.

Tactic #1: Good Books

Books are as close as our nearest Christian bookstore or library, where we find printed material on every subject. How-to books. Why-to books. How-I-did-it books and you-should books. *For many, they have become a substitute for God's voice.*

Tactic #2: Religious Broadcasts

The sounds of Christian evangelism are available by the snap of a TV or radio switch at any time of day or night. All proclaim "the truth." *For many people, they have become a substitute for God's voice.*

Tactic #3: Religious Services

One can attend a religious service almost any day of the week, most of them led by competent and spiritual people. Workshops and seminars, by experts on every conceivable subject, abound as church-affiliated activities. *For many people, they have become a substitute for God's voice.*

Tactic #4: Professional and spiritual counselors

These dedicated people are ready to give advice to anyone for a fee or at no cost at all. The best speakers on any subject can be heard on cassette for as little as $4.95. *For many people, they have become a substitute for God's voice.*

With all these substitute voices speaking of (and for) Christ, it is sometimes hard to see why we should take the trouble and time to establish our own personal relationship with the living Christ. We are much like the people of Israel who said to Moses, "You hear God for us."

To Christians today, people who write books and articles, preach on broadcasts, and give seminars can be helpful. However, we all need to be aware that the enemy wants to use these media as a substitute for God's voice speaking to us personally. They must be enhancers, a secondary resource, not the primary source of our life in the Spirit.

When we listen to friends, books, sermons, experts, we are making no commitment. We feel no real responsibility to act on what we hear. We can casually accept or reject the advice according to personal whim.

But when we hear from God himself, we must make a clear-cut decision. We have only two choices: to obey him or to disobey him.

God's Provision for Us to Hear Him Speak

If an individual were to become an adopted member of a family in another country and move there to spend the rest of his life, it would be necessary for him to learn the language of that new country. Otherwise, his inability to communicate would mean that his life would be severely limited and curtailed.

We have been made citizens of heaven, members of the family of God. Nothing is more important than learning to communicate with the Triune God who is our Father and our Savior and our Helper. Because hearing him speak is vital, God built into us a system that helps us concentrate upon things we deem as important and allows us to ignore those things that have little or no place in our value system.

God built into a portion of our brains a function that constantly

filters out unimportant information and focuses on what is meaningful to us. We call it the Reticular Activating System (RAS), and
this is the way it works:

1. *Positive focusing.* A new mother is so tuned in to her baby's
   needs that she can hear and respond to its every sound. In
   order to rest, she has to move the baby out of her room.
   Otherwise, every time the baby moves or sighs, the mother
   wakes up.
2. *Negative filtering.* People who live next to airports or railroad
   tracks after a while are no longer bothered by the noise of
   planes or shaking of the house as a train rumbles by.
3. *Individual perceiving.* If five people see an accident or look at the
   same scene, they will come up with completely different
   impressions.

Once your mind has decided something is important — like the
crying of a baby — the RAS will bring it to your attention every time.
Denis Waitley explains:

> The "Reticular Activating System" filters out the unimportant
> stimuli and focuses on what is important at the moment. . . . Once
> you have made a distinction that a certain value, thought, idea,
> sound, picture, or feeling is significant to you, your reticular acti-
> vating system is alerted. It immediately transmits any information
> it receives regarding this significant item into your consciousness.[8]

When you decide that hearing God is vital, your RAS starts putting God through whenever he speaks. You hear him with the same
intensity as a mother hears her newborn baby — and with the same
promptings to respond.

The RAS works to alert us regarding the spiritual world as we
hear our Lord speaking. It is our picker-and-chooser. As Waitley
describes it, the RAS is "the guardian of the mind."

Your Reticular Activating System records everything and will concentrate your attention on what you have previously programmed
to be important. If God's Word is of vital importance to you, your
RAS will put through all the messages that come to you from him.

8. Denis Waitley, *Seeds of Greatness* (New York, N.Y.: Pocket Books, 1983), pp. 123–124.

Two-way communication is essential to all relationships. Since hearing is your half of communication, you must learn to hear. The Lord created you and saved you for fellowship; you were called through God's faithfulness into fellowship with his Son Jesus Christ.

But fellowship is impossible without communion and communication! "God's voice must speak from within to bring enlightenment," says A. W. Tozer. "It must be the Spirit of God speaking soundlessly within — that is what brings him in and makes him accountable to God."[9]

Until your value system, your set of priorities, is so alerted that hearing God becomes your number-one priority, you are not going to hear him very well. Having you hear him is so important to God that he equipped you with the RAS to become attentive and tuned in to his voice. But if you are to develop a hearing ear, hearing God must be "vital" to you. Hearing him must have top priority in your life.

The Importance of Our Response

My eldest son lives in one of the most magnificent areas of Colorado, in a town surrounded by snow-capped peaks. Outside his office window is Pikes Peak, one of the most famous mountains in North America, seldom without snow and always majestic. People move to this area for the climate and the scenery. I never visit him without being overwhelmed by the wonder of it all.

One day, looking at the scenery with him and fearing there would come a day when he might not notice it, I said, "Richard, let me tell you how to protect yourself from taking this beauty for granted. When you see it, give expression to it: say something to someone about it, or write about it, or just say something out loud. You will then see more beauty than you have ever seen before."

We can easily lose the sensitivity to things that we once thought valuable. I live at one of the last frontiers of earth, Cape Kennedy. What an exciting place to be! Yet many residents here have become so accustomed to it that they have lost all appreciation, all excitement, all interest at being at the very edge of history.

9. A. W. Tozer, *Echoes from Eden* (Harrisburg, Penn.: Christian Publications, Inc., 1981), p. 62.

However, it is possible to develop an increasing awareness by properly applying the law of response available through our God-given RAS.

As noted previously, people who live next door to airports and are never bothered by the planes have used the *negative response* of filtering out what they don't want to hear. When they moved into the house, the noise of the planes was annoyingly loud, but they learned to ignore it and in a short time ceased to hear the sounds.

Conversely, the man who walks through the woods and hears the birds sing, and then tells you what birds he hears, is a man who has used a *positive response* — he focused his hearing by selective listening.

An uncle of mine took me through the woods one day and showed me sights I had never seen before, although I walked there often. Because my uncle always talked about what he saw, he saw more and more and was able to share it with me.

The person who listens to God and responds positively is someone who will hear more and more and more from the Lord. This is not because God is speaking more to that person, but because he or she has developed the ability to hear what God is saying.

Bearing Fruit with Perseverance

Our Lord encourages us beyond measure to listen to him: "For whoever has, to him shall more be given" (Matt. 13:12). A few verses later, Jesus explains that hard-seeming parable of the sower. The seed that fell into the good soil, he is telling us, are those who hear the word, understand it, and bear fruit (v. 23).

Now let us look at some practical suggestions on using the law of response to develop your ability to hear God.

1. There must be a *purposed response* — a commitment to respond. The first thing I told my son about staying sensitive to the beauty of his environment was: "Don't ever look at this without saying something about it. Don't let yourself look at it and not respond in some way."

There is a hardness that has settled over much of the church of Jesus Christ.

How did this take place? Not from a lack of hearing truth, but from a lack of responding to the truth we have heard. "Church," in whatever form we get it, directly or from the popular media, has become a performance. The result is a "hard heart" that no longer really hears.

The worst thing you can do — the quickest way to become insensitive — is to ignore an impression. So you must commit yourself to listening to your Lord for the purpose of responding to what he says, and you must not allow yourself to hear without responding.

2. There must be a *positive response.* The second advice I gave to Richard was: "Always give a positive response to what you see and observe. Say, 'What a beautiful peak! Look at the shadow of the trees! What a magnificent rock!' "

It is very important in developing a hearing heart that we give a positive response to what we hear from God. Responding positively is the key to developing sensitivity to God and to working discipline into our lives.

3. There must also be a *negative response.* As we practice developing our sensitivity to God's voice, negative responding is necessary in order to become insensitive and unresponsive to the world's values and ways.

Out of their wisdom and long experience, the Old Testament men of God recognized this truth when they told us: "Happy is the person who does not listen to the wicked, who does not go where sinners go, who does not do what bad people do" (cf. Ps. 1:1; Prov. 1:10; 4:14–15).

"Do not love the world nor the things in the world," counseled John (1 John 2:15). The world is passing away. And everything that people want in the world is passing away. But the person who does the will of God lives forever.

By deliberately ignoring the impressions of the world as much as possible, we can train ourselves to become less aware of its spiritually unhealthy distractions.

The world bombards us with the philosophy that "the good life" is measured by the abundance of material things one possesses. TV commercials, billboards, catalogs, alluring shop windows, and a thousand other devices tempt us to open our purses.

If we practice ignoring these stimuli by refusing to read catalogs or to expose ourselves to printed advertisements, turning off the media hype, and finding beneficial ways to amuse ourselves, we will slowly become less sensitized to "the things in the world." And

we can then spend time and money on things we truly need and
that God wants us to have.

4. There must be an *increased response*. The law of response says
our sensitivity increases in direct proportion to the positive re-
sponses we give to our impressions. The more we respond to the
things of God — especially to the guiding voice of the Holy Spirit —
the more aware we will become of him and *his* world.

5. There must be a *practical response*. The last advice I gave Richard
was: "If possible *do* something, act on what you have seen as soon
as possible. Share it with somebody, take a picture of it, write
something down about what you have noticed."

It should be the same when the Lord speaks. Your response
should include something practical and should be done as quickly
as is appropriate. For example:

1. If the Lord places in your mind a person who needs help, you
   should seek, as quickly as possible, to call, pray, write a letter,
   visit, or whatever type of action is appropriate.
2. If the Lord tells you to play with your child, you should do it
   at the earliest opportunity.
3. In reading the Bible, when the Holy Spirit guides you to see
   a truth, you should write it down and then respond specifically. Thus, if you read about hospitality, respond as quickly
   as possible by inviting someone over to eat or to fellowship
   in some other way.

To respond in a practical way to what God has said heightens
our sensitivity to his voice. But we cannot please God without faith,
and that begins with God's showing us something or telling us
something — and he does this in our imagination.

A. W. Tozer explains:

> Every advance made by mankind in any field began as an idea to
> which nothing for the time corresponded. The mind of the inventor
> simply took bits of familiar ideas and made out of them something
> which was not only wholly unfamiliar but which up to that time was
> altogether nonexistent. Thus we "created" things and by so doing
> prove ourselves to have been made in the image of the Creator.[10]

10. A. W. Tozer, *Born After Midnight* (Harrisburg, Penn.: Christian Publications, Inc.,
1959), p. 92.

A purified and Spirit-controlled imagination is . . .
   the sacred gift of seeing,
   the ability to peer
beyond the veil
and gaze with astonished wonder
upon the beauties and mysteries
   of things holy and eternal.[11]

11. Ibid. p. 94 (adapted).

As, down in the sunless retreats of the ocean,
  Sweet flowers are springing no mortal can see,
So, deep in my heart, the still prayer of devotion,
  Unheard by the world, rises, silent, to Thee.
      My God! silent, to Thee —
      Pure, warm, silent, to Thee.

As, still to the star of its worship, though clouded,
  The needle points faithfully o'er the dim sea,
So, dark as I roam, through this wintry world shrouded,
  The hope of my spirit turns, trembling, to Thee,
      My God! trembling to Thee —
      True, fond, trembling, to Thee.[1]

---

1. Thomas Moore, 1719–1852

2

A Pure Heart

Y̲ou and I also need pure, undivided hearts if we would hear God.

"Pure." To most of us the word means the absence of contamination, the elimination of evil. But this is only part of its meaning. The other part is single-mindedness — the desire and commitment to one thing, one purpose.

"Pure gold" is gold that is not only free from dirt; it is gold that is free from anything else, even the best of other materials. Even a ring that contains gold, silver, and diamonds is not pure gold. For pure gold *is* gold — nothing more, nothing less than that one element.

Similarly, a pure heart is a heart that wills and seeks and wants one thing only. Every decision, every choice, every evaluation, is based on that one desire. Sören Kierkegaard titled one of his books *Purity of Heart Is to Will One Thing*.

We might say that "the heart" is the real person. It is "pure" when all the pretense, masks, regulated behavior, old concepts and guards, are stripped away. And there is no question as to the importance to God of a pure heart:

1. God's *promise* to a group of his people in captivity was: "And you will seek Me and find Me, when you search for Me with all your heart" (Jer. 29:13).
2. God's *desire* for his people is expressed in the fact that the Lord searches all the earth for people who have given themselves completely to him.
3. God's *admonition* to us through James is: Give yourselves to

45

me. Resist the devil and he will flee from you. Come near to me, and I will come near to you. You are sinners. So clean sin out of your lives. Purify your hearts. (cf. James 4:7–8) In other words, we are trying to follow God and the world at the same time and must avoid such double-minded behavior. Our hearts must be pure with a desire to follow God only.

How Do We Get a Pure Heart?

If a pure heart is so important to God, how do we cooperate with God so that we attain this purity of purpose? The process takes time and action on our part, but is guided by the Holy Spirit in the life of the sincere, cooperative believer. And it includes definite procedures.

Procedure #1: Cleansing

Do you know the difference between forgiveness and cleansing? It's the difference between cutting off a weed at the ground with your mower and pulling it out by its roots. Forgiveness has to do with the results of sin. Cleansing has to do with the *cause* of sin.

Forgiveness comes by confession and restitution. Cleansing comes by walking in the light: "God is light; in him there is no darkness.... If we say that we have fellowship with Him and yet walk in the darkness, we lie and do not practice the truth; but if we walk in the light as He Himself is in the light, we have fellowship with one another, and the blood of Jesus His Son cleanses us from all sin" (1 John 1:5–7).

Many of us keep asking God for forgiveness for the same sins, over and over and over again. The reason is that we have never experienced cleansing. The cause of the sins has not been eradicated.

If the top of the sin-weed is cut off, for a short while it cannot be seen on the surface. But the weed will soon be back again, unless it is pulled out by its root. When we keep committing certain sins, we need to ask God to show us the root, the cause of our disobedience. We must ask him what our part is in getting rid of it.

To "walk in the light" means that the Lord will be asking you to make a lifestyle change. This may mean a change in the way you use time — a form of discipline or some new and ordered behavior that he wishes to integrate into your life.

Parents punish their children for a short time period in a way they think best. "But God," says the writer to the Hebrews as the Spirit dictated, "disciplines us for our good, that we may share His holiness. All discipline for the moment seems not to be joyful, but sorrowful; yet to those who have been trained by it, afterwards it yields the peaceful fruit of righteousness" (Heb. 12:10–11).

A cleansed heart is the first step toward a pure heart.

Procedure #2: Circumcision

What is a circumcised heart? How do I get one? What will be its results?

First remember that all the physical rules of the Old Testament were just shadows of spiritual realities. This is sometimes hard to understand, but Paul clearly spells it out in his letter to the Romans: "A person is not a true Jew if he is only a Jew in his physical body. True circumcision is not only on the outside of the body. "For he is not a Jew who is one outwardly; neither is circumcision that which is outward in the flesh. But he is a Jew who is one inwardly; and circumcision is that which is of the heart, by the Spirit, not by the letter; and his praise is not from men but from God." (Rom. 2:28–29).

If you have ever seen a person whose whole life was wrapped up in anything, surrounded by and entwined in that one thing over a continuing period of time, you will begin to get a picture of a "whole" heart. A circumcised heart has had everything superfluous cut away, and that means removing the "good" that hinders the "best."

Cleansing takes care of evil roots. Circumcision takes care of the good but unnecessary things that crowd out God. When we understand this, we realize we need some very delicate and deep surgery in our hearts. That surgery will place God in a position of priority that no other person, thing, or pursuit can ever know.

How does this take place?

There is, as in all other things, a twofold effort — God's and ours. We cannot do it without him, and he will not do it without our cooperation:

1. Our part: Circumcise then your heart. "Circumcise yourselves to the LORD and remove the foreskins of your heart, men of Judah and inhabitants of Jerusalem . . ." (Jer. 4:4).
2. God's part: "Moreover the LORD your God will circumcise your heart and the heart of your descendants, to love the LORD your God with all your heart and with all your soul, in order that you may live" (Deut. 30:6).

As in every other phase of the Christian life, heart circumcision is a cooperative action between God and ourselves.

Some Practical Suggestions

1. Tell God you want a pure heart and are willing to cooperate with him.
2. Tell him you love the praise of man too much and ask him to deliver you from this.
3. Ask him to tell you the first step he wants you to take with him.
4. Listen and obey.

God's promise is: "Blessed are the pure in heart, for they shall see God" (Matt. 5:8).

If your heart is pure, your perception of God will be clear and definite, and communication with him will be easier.

A *hearing ear.* A *pure heart.* These two are the basic necessities for God's child to hear the Father speak.

2

Clearing Away the Clutter

An unquestioned fact:

> We all, beholding the Lord,
> shall be changed into his likeness.

A step-by-step process:

> from glory to glory

Supported by the Holy Spirit:

> by the Spirit of the Lord

The key:

> beholding
>> not ancient Hebrew history
>> not marvelously intriguing stories
>
> beholding
>> the LORD and the qualities of his character.[1]

---

1. 2 Corinthians 3:18, adapted by Peter M. Lord.

3

The Traps

The road to effective communion with God is pitted and pebbled with obstacles and mined with dangerous deceptions that can cause you to stumble and fall. These are many traps that Satan, the enemy, sets to catch the unwary child of God.

This clutter — these hindrances — can keep you from hearing God, from distinguishing his voice and having the fellowship with him that is your privilege as his child. For your safe travel on this journey, it is important that you understand the dangers and learn how to avoid them.

The Trap of Hurry and Busyness

This trap is a lifestyle that does not allow time to stop and listen to God and commune with him. There seem to be so many good things to do that there is hardly a minute left to speak and listen to God. The attitude, often subconscious and unspoken, is that if God has anything to say, he had better hurry.

You surely know people caught in this trap. You may even be one yourself. Busy people. Religious people. Overcommitted people. The let's-hurry-up-with-prayer-so-we-can-get-on-with-it people.

It's like going to the doctor's office, telling him (or her) all your symptoms, and then leaving before he or she can make a diagnosis and tell you what to do. Dr. Richard Foster, in *Celebration of Discipline*, reminds us that "hurry is not *of* the devil, it *is* the devil."

If you have gotten into this trap, there is a way out. It begins with an understanding that the Lord wants your love and fellowship before anything else. Knowing that intimacy can never be hurried and rushed, you set a time in your life for meeting God and make it of primary importance. Many people have found an early-morning hour the best and easiest time for this fellowship with God.

You can hear God better when you give him quality time.

The Trap of External Distractions

Most people learning a new skill know they must give it their full attention because they are in an area of unfamiliarity. Beginners in the art of hearing God's voice are particularly prone to external distraction. Generally they have a great need for quietude because they are so sensitively attuned to the outer world and are very conscious of it.

External noises or activities that might distract include TV, radio, and others' talking or playing. Other attention-diverting activities could be doing something else while trying to hear God, such as vacuuming, driving, or cooking.

Entering into silence is an effort that requires complete concentration. If you are a beginner, external distractions must be reduced to a minimum to enable you to begin to be conscious of the One who dwells in your inner world.

During a normal day, God's communication with you will blossom out of the quiet time spent earlier with him. Without it, the Lord withdraws until you stop and give him your full attention. There is never a time in this pilgrimage when focusing on him is not necessary. The way out of this particular problem is fairly simple for those who are willing to pay the price of time and concentration.

Jesus knew about the trap of distractions. That was one reason he said, "When you pray, go into your inner room, and when you have shut your door, pray to your Father who is in secret, and your Father who sees in secret will repay you" (Matt. 6:6).

Jesus — the perfect Son of God — gave a demonstration of this need for quiet, for getting away from the world. "But he himself would often slip away to the wilderness and pray" (Luke 5:16).

Like Jesus, in your early-day "wilderness," you will find solitude both from noise and activity. Here are some practical suggestions:

1. Early in the morning seems to be the best time to find a place free from noise and activity. While other members of the family are asleep, you can get alone with God.
2. If a husband and wife are making this spiritual journey at the same time, they should arrange to be in separate rooms.
3. Good places to choose (assuming that there is no one else in the room) are the dining room table or a couch or desk in the den.
4. Creative alternatives to a home setting would be to go to your office early and spend the time there alone. Or to a church. One of the quietest, least-used places in our city is the small chapel of the local hospital.
5. Try to use the same place all the time. Any uniqueness of the setting will soon wear off and will not demand your attention.

Filtering out external distractions will help you focus on what God wants to tell you.

The Trap of Not Recognizing God's Voice

One of the common problems people have is not being able to recognize the voice of God when they hear it. They do not know him; consequently his voice is unfamiliar to them.

There is a delightful story in the Old Testament about Samuel's first experience with hearing the voice of the Lord. Young Samuel was learning about God in the temple and was assisting Eli. He did not recognize God speaking to him until Eli enlightened him:

...And word from the LORD was rare in those days, visions were infrequent.

And it happened at that time as Eli was lying down in his place (now his eyesight had begun to grow dim and he could not see well), and the lamp of God had not yet gone out, and Samuel was lying down in the temple of the LORD where the ark of God was, that the LORD called Samuel; and he said,"Here I am."

Then he ran to Eli and said, "Here I am, for you called me." But he said, "I did not call, lie down again." So he went and lay down.

And the LORD called yet again, "Samuel!" So Samuel arose and went to Eli, and said, "Here I am, for you called me." But he answered, "I did not call, my son, lie down again."

Now Samuel did not yet know the LORD, nor had the word of the LORD yet been revealed to him.

So the LORD called Samuel again for the third time. And he arose and went to Eli, and said, "Here I am, for you called me." Then Eli discerned that the LORD was calling the boy.

And Eli said to Samuel, "Go lie down, and it shall be if He calls you, that you shall say 'Speak, LORD, for Thy servant is listening.' " So Samuel went and lay down in his place.

Then the LORD came and stood and called as at other times, "Samuel! Samuel!" And Samuel said, "Speak, for Thy servant is listening" (1 Sam. 3:1–10).

Not recognizing God's voice is more common among beginners, learners like Samuel. Either they have no idea about God and his manner of speaking or they have preconceived ideas that are wrong. One of the most common experiences I have in encouraging people to listen to God is that they hear him but cannot believe that it is really the Lord communicating with them.

The more you get to know God, the more you recognize his voice.

The Trap of Our Mind Set

In addition to not recognizing God's voice, even when he is speaking directly to us, there is the problem of mind set. We are usually ready to hear God when he speaks through a great preacher or important author, but sometimes God speaks through people we least expect him to use.

I was planning a trip to Disney World for my eight-year-old son, John. My idea was to include a group of parents and children. That way I would have other adults to visit with, and John would have his peers to play with on the excursion.

For a week I issued invitations, only to have each family decline for one reason or another.

"What's wrong?" I wondered aloud at the supper table.

My sixteen-year-old daughter tossed her head and said, "Daddy, maybe God's speaking to you. Maybe he wants just you and John to go — alone."

It took me a whole week to recognize that Ruthie was right, because my mind set was not that God would speak to me through her. But he certainly did! God was telling me I should let it be a special time just for John and myself.

If God could speak through a donkey to Balaam, he can speak through anybody to us. Once you get to know him so well that you know his voice, you will also know he can speak in many ways and through anybody.

You will be more sensitive to God's voice in all situations and among all people if you do not predetermine the most likely place to hear it.

The Trap of Trying Too Hard

Trying to rush the process is a common fault among people who are concentrating intensely on learning something important.

I remember learning to snow-ski. I was trying too hard, concentrating too much. The result was that I fell, over and over again. I paid too little attention to the instructor's repeated advice: "Relax. Let your skis do the work for you."

Like me in my skiing efforts, beginners in listening to God often feel they must succeed right away. Fearing they might not hear something really important, they fall into the trap of trying too hard. In what they perceive to be an emergency situation, people often believe that they must have an answer "Right now!" Waiting on God can be difficult when the pressures mount and a "crisis" seems imminent.

But this is one way Satan traps us, and it needs to be guarded against. We need to "still" ourselves in meditation by remembering that God is in control. He knows all about the "emergency." We should realize that our only responsibility is to listen with an open heart to receive whatever the Lord wants to say.

By recalling God's faithfulness in the past and his promises of guidance, we can learn to wait patiently for his answers.

The Trap of Presumption

Sometimes we assume that something is *probably* true, without proof that it is. If we make the supposition that we already know what God is going to say or do in a given situation, we are drawing an inner conclusion — presuming — that we do not really need to listen to him.

The Old Testament story of how the Gibeonites managed to deceive Joshua and the leaders of Israel (Joshua 9) is a perfect example of presumption.

The Israelites were cocksure after crossing the Jordan and achieving victories at Jericho and Ai. Hadn't they successfully conquered the Promised Land? How confident they now were that they could handle things!

Then they were approached by the wily people of Gibeon, who had seen and heard how God had given the Israelites victory. Craftily the Gibeonite delegation lied, pretending they had come from a far country and wanted nothing more than a covenant of peace and to be of service.

In a victory mood, the overconfident Israelites looked at the Gibeonites' worn-out sandals and clothes, the weary donkeys, the old wineskins. What the visitors said and the way they looked matched, so the men of Israel *presumed* that everything was all right. *And they did not ask the counsel of the* Lord (Josh. 9:14). They went ahead on their own! Joshua made a treaty with them, a covenant to let them live in peace.

Too late the Israelites realized what they had done! A few days later, when they learned that the Gibeonites actually lived nearby and thus the Israelites had disobeyed God's specific command, there was nothing they could do, since they had vowed not to harm them. Their presumption resulted in a very bad mistake, which was to affect Israel for years to come.

How easy in times of great victory and continuous winning, to shift from God-reliance to self-reliance and a know-it-all attitude. Situations where God has blessed over and over again in a certain way tend to become routine to us. *It is easy to shift from faith in God to faith in a method or past experience.* But, to bring our faith back to him, God will often allow us to fail, as he did Joshua and the Israelites of old.

Beware of the traps of presumption!

Presumption Trap #1: "It Worked for Others . . ."

We often tell ourselves, "God blessed that way of doing it before, so that's how we will do it now."

When God has blessed others by using certain methods, we sometimes presume that *we* should use the same methods. We don't realize that God blessed that way for others because that's the way he had ordered them to do things.

Nowhere is this more common than in church programs. One church prays and receives an answer — a specific method of carrying out a certain order of God. God gives a way; they follow it. And they are richly blessed because God blesses what God orders.

Then another church, seeing this blessing, copies the program — because they believe God is blessing the program itself. They fail to realize that what he is really blessing is *obedience*. And they never stop to ask him, "Father, what do you want *us* to do?"

Presumption Trap #2: "I Know My Own Strengths . . ."

Do you sometimes tell yourself, "There is no reason to listen to God about this, when I already know I can perform well"?

One of the greatest areas of presumption is in what we think of as our "strengths" — an area in which we are confident that we are able. However, we may not really be strong in an area yet are deceived into thinking we are. This is called a "perceived strength". Presumption prevents us from even wanting to hear what God or anyone else says.

How can we deal with "perceived strengths" that prevent hearing what the Lord would say to us?

First, there must be a total acceptance of Jesus' statement that "Apart from Me you can do *nothing*" (John 15:5).

Is this true? Or is this an exaggerated interpretation of Christ's meaning? Our Lord was not referring to the physical world but to the spiritual. He meant that in the spiritual realm, *by yourself*, you can do nothing.

If this is written deeply upon the tables of your heart, then you will operate on the basis that you need the Lord at all times.

Second, you must become aware of those areas in which you move without contacting the Lord simply because you are sure *you* can handle the situation. Guarding against the presumption of "perceived strengths" can have varying applications:

a) *In the area of our talent(s) or work*. Here, because we *do* have real strength, we may forget we need guidance.

Recently a young man in our church was about to give his first message. His palms were wet when we shook hands, and he said, "I've spent a lot of time with the Lord over this message — and I'm still nervous."

"You're in a good position to trust the Lord," I told him. "I've been preaching for thirty-five years and it seems easier for me to preach...."

"Yeah," he answered. "I guess I'll be that way, too, eventually."

"You misunderstood," I said. "I didn't finish. I was saying that it's relatively easy for me to preach because I sometimes think I can do all right without the Lord's help."

"Oh," he agreed, beginning to understand.

"You see," I continued, "I can speak a message — even a worthwhile message that the listeners enjoy — without asking any help from the Lord. The big question is: 'What would it accomplish spiritually? Would it reach hearts to bring about redemption?' "

The young man nodded his head slowly as I went on; "A message I preached on my own wouldn't have much eternal value. That's why I said you're in a good position to trust the Lord. You know you need his guidance."

b) *In an area we believe we're strong — when we're not.* The point here is to know we need help and when and from whom we should seek it.

Parenting would be such an area, for parents with small children often *assume* they know what to do and exactly how to do it. Everything seems to go well for the ten or twelve years they are able to force the children to do what they want.

But there comes a day — often in the teenage years — when the parents begin to experience certain things with their children they can no longer handle. Then they seek help from the "experts." How often the help they get deals only with their specific parenting weaknesses.

If the parents had only understood from the beginning that they needed God's help — if they had sought it on a daily basis — they would have had a different situation when the children began to express their growing independence.

Many times our lack of expertise is not discovered until we are a good way down the line. It is hard to explain anything to those who believe they are experts. Need and real dependence make for good listeners and seekers after God's help. Here are some practical suggestions:

Make a list of your perceived strengths.

Confess to the Lord that you have a tendency to operate in these areas without his help.

Ask the Holy Spirit to give you a warning (that "still small voice") when you are moving in your own strength.

Make an extra special effort to seek God's mind in these areas.

One of the best examples of this I know is Danny Daniels, our Minister of Counseling. Danny has walked with the Lord a long time and has been a counselor for all kinds of problems. Many people testify to the help he has given them.

But Danny says, "I can't use the same answers for everybody. I must stay open to the Lord's leading every minute I'm counseling somebody. One way I do it is by praying before each session, giving it, myself, and the other person to the Lord. I ask for guidance according to where the person is and what the Lord wants me to do. I stick close to Scripture, too. That keeps me depending on him, instead of what I might have learned elsewhere."

c) *In the area(s) where we have strong feelings or opinions.* If we are not on the alert, it is easy to *presume* that God agrees with us.

"Be on the alert," the Holy Spirit warns us through the apostle Peter. "Your adversary, the devil, prowls about like a roaring lion, seeking someone to devour" (1 Peter 5:8).

The apostle Paul cautions us that Satan even disguises himself as an angel of light (2 Cor. 11:14).

God wants you to understand that the adversary will come to you in disguise, with the intent of deceiving you. Your own feelings and opinions cannot be trusted in this kind of situation, any more than could the feelings and opinions of Joshua and the Israelites so long ago.

But you can trust God. And he has said, "I will never desert you. Nor will I ever forsake you" (Heb. 13:5b).

So we can lift up our heads with confidence and say with the psalmist: "The Lord is my helper, I shall not be afraid." (Ps. 54:4; 56:3, 11). God has made it possible for you and me to stay on the alert. To keep in communion with him. To be dependent on him.

There are four general precepts that will help you focus on what God is saying, thus giving you greater wisdom and strength to recognize and avoid the traps of the enemy:

1. There is no need to be "uptight" in this matter, but there *is* a need to be sober and make sure that your mind is set on the Lord.
2. Take the necessary time to wait patiently for the Lord to advise and answer you.
3. Since God blesses faith, be sure you look at *him* and not to your own opinions or others' past experiences.
4. Remember, most of all, that "God moves in a mysterious way his wonders to perform."[2] The Lord shows us many unexpected applications of his eternal wisdom and power.

Satan's traps are many, and they can catch or stop us unawares. He also has snares — those major, deceptively attractive things by which God's child is too often entangled, involved in difficulties, or impeded. The next chapter will reveal some of Satan's more insidious tactics against the Christian.

---

2. William Cowper, "God Moves in a Mysterious Way."

For the error bred in the bone
    Of each woman and each man
Craves what it cannot have;
    Not universal love
But to be loved alone.

Auden

I have loved you
    with an everlasting love.

I have drawn you
    with lovingkindness.

The Lord God
(Jer. 31:3)

A new commandment I give you:
    love one another.
As I have loved you, so must you
    love one another.

Jesus Christ
(John 13:34)

4

The Snares

In the last chapter, we looked at some relatively minor traps the enemy has prepared for the unwary child of God on this road to communion with God. Now we will consider some major impediments — the snares.

The Snare of Rebellion

Rebellion is defined by one dictionary as "opposition to one in authority or dominance...."

Scripture calls rebellion "sin." It is a deliberate refusal to do what is known indisputably to be the will of God and involves the choice not to obey his authority. The sin of rebellion is a decision to do what *you* want, not what God wants.

There is another type of sin in the Scriptures called "transgression" — a fall or mistake, sin done in weakness or carelessness. For example, an individual, in a moment of weakness, could lose his temper and say cruel or unkind things to someone else. This would be a "transgression."

However, if — when the Holy Spirit convicts him and orders him to apologize and ask forgiveness — the sinner refuses to do so, the "transgression" becomes "rebellion" against God. Then he has a major problem with his communication and fellowship with the Lord.

A pastor learning to listen to the Lord wrote to me not long ago. He said:

As I was driving down the road one morning, God clearly spoke to my inner being: "Give five hundred dollars to a family in your church that really needs it. Do it anonymously by Christmas."

There was no doubt in my heart that it was God's voice, but the amount was so large for our budget that I said to God, "If You really want me to do this, confirm Your word to me."

Brother, for three hours all communication was cut off between the Father and me. I prayed continually, but I knew God was not honoring my prayers. It was as if God were deliberately ignoring me as I talked to Him.

I was beginning to get frantic about not knowing what that meant. At the end of three hours, God gently spoke to me again. He said, "Son, why did you ask Me to confirm My word to you? You know My voice. You knew it was I the first time."

Needless to say, I repented, and fellowship was reestablished.

This pastor was right. If you know God is speaking, it is rebellious to do anything other than obey. However, if you are honestly not sure it is God's voice, it is all right to ask for confirmation.

On one occasion, God taught Saul and those with him how important obedience is. He wants you and me to understand the same lesson shown us in 1 Samuel 15.

God had sent his anointed king, Saul, to punish the Amalekites. His command was succinct and to the point: "Utterly destroy all that he has, and do not spare him" (v. 3).

King Saul and the Israelites won a great victory. But they captured King Agag alive. And they destroyed everything except the best of the sheep, the oxen, the lambs — sparing all things they considered valuable. Then they waited for the prophet Samuel to come and celebrate the victory with thanksgiving to God.

Instead of rejoicing with them, Samuel denounced King Saul in the name of the Lord. "Has the LORD as much delight in burnt offerings and sacrifices," he asked, "as in obeying the voice of the Lord?" (v. 22a).

This was Samuel speaking in the name of the Lord to King Saul — and to us today. His irrefutable answer thunders down through time: "Behold, to obey is better than sacrifice, and to hearken than the fat of rams. For rebellion is as the sin of divination, and stubbornness [insubordination] is as iniquity and idolatry . . ." (vv. 22b–23a).

Certain words really jump out:

To obey is better than sacrifice

Could this mean that obedience is better than going out on visitation or teaching Sunday-school class?

Does this mean that in God's sight rebellion is as bad as witchcraft or dealing in the occult?

Is God really putting insubordination in the same class as iniquity and idol worship?

Yes, that's what he says!

In the New Testament, God uses the writer of Hebrews to explain further: "For if we go on sinning willfully after receiving the knowledge of the truth, there no longer remains a sacrifice for sins, but a certain terrifying expectation of judgment, and the fury of a fire which will consume the adversaries" (Heb. 10:26–27). Above all, this passage of Scripture is saying that sinning willfully is bad since one has thereby ". . . trampled under foot the Son of God, and has regarded as unclean the blood of the covenant by which he was sanctified, and has insulted the Spirit of grace" (v 29).

Each one of us has the responsibility to obey and see to it that individually we do not refuse the holy God who is speaking to us — ". . . For if those did not escape when they refused him who warned them on earth, much less shall we escape who turn away from Him who warns from heaven" (Heb. 12:25).

The psalmist recognized that we need to maintain a spirit of submission. "The sacrifices of God are a broken spirit . . ." his prayer reminds us. Then, turning his full attention to God, he confirms what he has just said: ". . . A broken and a contrite heart, O God, Thou wilt not despise" (Ps. 51:17).

"Thus says the Lord," the prophet Isaiah tells us — " 'Heaven is My throne, and the earth is My footstool. Where then is a house you could build for Me? And where is a place that I may rest? For My hand made all these things, thus all these things came into being,' declares the Lord" (Isa. 66:1–2a).

Then, because God knows our hearts — because he knows we want to please him — he defines for us the people he is pleased with: "But to this one I will look, to him who is humble and contrite of spirit, and who trembles at my word" (Isa. 66:2b).

God is looking for those who tremble at his words because they will obey what he is saying. He asks us through James, "Do you think that the Scripture speaks to no purpose: 'He jealously desires the spirit which He has made to dwell in us'?" (James 4:5). Then comes the answer:

> But He gives a greater grace. Therefore it says, "God is opposed to the proud, but gives grace to the humble." Submit therefore to God. Resist the devil and he will flee from you. Draw near to God and he will draw near to you. Cleanse your hands, you sinners; and purify your hearts, you double-minded. Be miserable and mourn and weep; let your laughter be turned into mourning, and your joy to gloom. Humble yourselves in the presence of the Lord, and he will exalt you" (James 4:6–10).

Here are two practical suggestions to help you avoid the sin of disobedience:

1. If you cannot get answers from the Lord, check to see if the enemy has caught you in his snare of rebellion and arrogance.
2. Ask yourself whether there is a point where God told you to do something and you did not. If so, take care of it immediately.

The Snare of Double-Mindedness

A spiritually double-minded person is an individual who has not made up his mind to do God's will, accept God's advice, or believe God's evaluation, no matter what it may be.

Oh, yes, this person does want to hear from God! But, after he has heard, he will make up his mind as to whether or not to follow what God says.

This is not God's way. He tells us through James: "If any of you lacks wisdom, let him ask of God, who gives to all men generously and without reproach, and it will be given to him" (James 1:5).

For example, a person seeking God's counsel about restoring a broken relationship with another person might receive words like this from the Father: "My child, this relationship is what it is because of you and the things you have said. You need to go to the other person and ask forgiveness. Confess your wrong without saying one word about his part in it."

Since it is unlikely that a double-minded person would carry out such advice, God — who knows our hearts — might not give him an answer. James tells us that we must ask in faith, with no doubting. Although God has invited us to ask him for wisdom, there is also this warning:

> But let him ask in faith without any doubting, for the one who doubts is like the surf of the sea driven and tossed by the wind. For let not that man expect that he will receive anything from the Lord, being a double-minded man, unstable in all his ways. (James 1:6–8)

If you are not sure that God will keep his promise — if you are afraid of what God's answer might be, if you have an area of your life not fully turned over to him or one in which you have strong desires and opinions of your own — then you will approach him with doubt, not faith.

To overcome this double-mindedness, you first need to acknowledge your fears. You must realize that you alone are responsible for your being double-minded, and you must be determined to do something about it. As with all sin, you must acknowledge that your doubts and vacillations are wrong. Only then will you escape the snare of double-mindedness.

You and I are faced with the same decision with which Joshua confronted the children of Israel: "And if it is disagreeable in your sight to serve the Lord, choose for yourselves today whom you will serve: whether the gods which your fathers served which were beyond the River, or the gods of the Amorites in whose land you are living; but as for me and my house, we will serve the Lord" (Josh. 24:15).

Jesus has promised, "If any man is willing to do His will, he shall know of the teaching, whether it is of God, or whether I speak from Myself" (John 7:17).

In the vacuum left by our not hearing God's voice, the enemy speaks the words he wants us to hear. These words are often exactly what we have longed to hear, since they seem to suit our purposes and desires. But individually, each for him or herself, we must make a deliberate decision in our hearts to do anything God wants done and to accept in faith any advice or solution he gives. Simply put, being single-minded is like signing a check, giving it to God and letting him fill in what he wants you to do.

The Snare of Pretense

A pretense is an act of make-believe, a fiction, a claim made or implied so as to give a false appearance. "Hypocritical" is a word used to describe people who are pretentious. They feign qualities they do not have.

No group of people received a more serious rebuke from the Lord Jesus than those he labeled "hypocrites." Enough is said in Scripture about hypocrites to guarantee that if our behavior closely resembles theirs, we will have a problem with hearing from God.

Our Lord abhors pretense. "Because this people draw near with their words and honor Me, with their lip service, but they remove their hearts far from Me and their reverence for Me consists of tradition learned by rote" (Isa. 29:13).

In 2 Corinthians 3:13–18, the word *veil* is used to indicate hypocrisy. Moses is depicted as wearing a veil, or covering, to hide the fact that the glory of God was fading from his face. With the veil over his face, Moses was pretending to be more in touch with God than he really was.

The Scriptures declare that "But whenever a man turns to the Lord, the veil is taken away. Now the Lord is the Spirit; and where the Spirit of the Lord is, there is liberty. But we all with unveiled face beholding as in a mirror the glory of the Lord, are being transformed into the same image from glory to glory, just as from the Lord, the Spirit" (2 Cor. 3:16–18).

The advantage of an unveiled face, of being a non-pretentious person, is to reflect God's glory as we are being transformed into the likeness of Jesus.

Hypocrisy manifests itself in many ways:

1. By Christians who pretend to be right with God when they are not. They hope to impress others with their piety. But their pretense, with a smile or a "praise the Lord" or "I'm doing fine," goes both manward and Godward.
2. By persons with low self-esteem, who feel they must meet certain standards to be accepted by others.
3. By those who have an image or status they perceive must be maintained. Often, Christian workers who have troubles — but believe that Christian workers are somehow exempt from problems — will wear a veil to maintain their "credibility."

People whose acceptance by others is their top priority will wear the appropriate veils or "masks" to fit the occasion and their own weaknesses.

How can we guard against and cure the common Christian malady of pretense? First, you and I must recognize God's disdain for pretense, and we must also understand the problems we bring into our relationship with God when we pretend. Next, as we acknowledge God's love for honesty and his intense desire to help those in need, we come to realize that he helps us because he sees behind the mask to our real needs and knows us as we really are. Finally, if we show weakness, meet failure, or fall into sin, we must come to see that it is our position in Christ that makes us acceptable to God and not our behavior.

Here are two practical suggestions for avoiding the snare of pretense:

1. Be honest with God in prayer. Tell him how you are and how you feel and ask his help.
2. When God sends people to help you, be honest with them, accepting them as his representatives. Take off your mask! To be dishonest with someone God sends is to be dishonest with the Lord.

You and I are so used to wearing masks with people that we wear them all the time. Sometimes when I'm reading, I skip over lengthy quotations, but I'd like you to read this one, since it explains so clearly why we hide our true feelings from others:

> Don't be fooled by me. Don't be fooled by the face I wear. I wear a mask. I wear a thousand masks — masks that I am afraid to take off; and none of them are me.
>
> Pretending is an art that is second nature to me, but don't be fooled. For my sake, don't be fooled. I give the impression that I am secure, that all is sunny and unruffled within me as well as without; that confidence is my name and coolness my game, that the water is calm and I am in command; and that I need no one. But don't believe me, please. My surface may seem smooth, but my surface is my mask, my ever varying and ever concealing mask.
>
> Beneath lies no smugness, no complacence. Beneath dwells the real me in confusion, in fear, in aloneness. But I hide that. I don't want anybody to know it. I panic at the thought of my weakness and

fear being exposed. That's why I frantically create a mask to hide behind — a nonchalant, sophisticated facade — to help me pretend, to shield me from the glance that knows. But such a glance is precisely my salvation, my only salvation, and I know it. That is, if it's followed by acceptance; if it's followed by love.

It's the only thing that can liberate me from myself, from my own self-built prison wall, from the barriers I so painstakingly erect. It's the only thing that will assure me of what I can't assure myself — that I am really something. . . .

Who am I, you may wonder. I am someone you know very well. I am every man you meet. I am every woman you meet. I am every child you meet. I am right in front of you. Please . . . love me.[1]

Seeing yourself as you really are will help you to unmask. It will take away the desire and need for a veil of pretense and hypocrisy. According to God's Word, what you really are *right now* is — a child of God! When you become honest with the Lord and see yourself as his child, you will truly know the love that will separate you from all pretense.

Love and acceptance is a sure cure for hypocrisy. We can joyfully remove our masks, not having the need to pretend anymore. That is why John the Beloved (isn't that a revealing name?) emphasizes "For this is the message you have heard from the beginning, that we should love each other" (1 John 3:11).

The apostle Paul tells us that just as we are accepted by God through his beloved Son, he expects us to love and accept each other (Eph. 1:3–6; Rom. 15:7).

We have looked in this chapter at three major snares Satan uses as roadblocks on our walk with Christ: rebellion, double-mindedness, and pretense. We will next consider some spiritual hindrances that slow our journey as Christians and deafen our ears to what God is saying.

1. Denis Waitley, *Seeds of Greatness* (Old Tappan, N.J.: Fleming H. Revell, 1983), pp. 32, 33.

Nought have I else to do;
    I sing the whole day long;
And He whom most I love to please,
    Doth listen to my song;
He caught and bound my wandering wing,
    But still He bends to hear me sing.

My cage confines me round;
    Abroad I cannot fly;
But though my wing is closely bound,
    My heart's at liberty.
My prison walls cannot control
    The light, the freedom of the soul.

Oh! it is good to soar
    These bolts and bars above,
To Him whose purpose I adore,
    Whose providence I love,
And in thy mighty will to find
    The joy, the freedom of the mind.[1]

1. Madame Jeanne Guyon, from "A Little Bird I Am," *Union With God* (Augusta, Maine: Christian Books, 1981), p. 102.

5

The Hindrances

A "hindrance" is something that slows or makes difficult our progress. It holds us back. It delays, impedes, or prevents action.

Let us look now at some of the hindrances the enemy uses against the child of God.

The first two are "internal distractions" — processes that can invade and dilute the spiritual life of a believer. The third "hindrance" is perhaps the most dangerous weapon of the enemy. It reflects a deep void — an absence of spiritual life — in professed Christians who have not yet truly heard God's message of salvation.

The Hindrance of Runaway Emotions

At 11:00 one night, quite by accident, I discovered that my son had sneaked away from the house through the window of his room. Immediately, my emotions began to run high. I was angry and very tired, and this was inconvenient, to say the least. I was also afraid of what might happen to him.

It is at times like these that a parent needs to hear from God, both for inner peace and in order to be able to give the right discipline. An inappropriate reaction by a parent to a child's misbehavior is just as wrong as the child's behavior and perhaps more destructive.

But there was no way I could hear from God as long as anger

and fear were banging around inside my head. And sometimes, when we most need to hear from God, we least want to.

It took me nearly two hours, while waiting for John to come home, to get quiet enough for me to hear the Lord say, "Peter, don't discipline him tonight. Wait until tomorrow, when you have a clear mind."

I did wait until the next day. The guidance I received from the Lord in dealing with John was far different from what I had anticipated. The Lord told me to give John a full pardon this time, without punishment. Then I was to explain to him what grace is.

The results of disciplining John God's way showed some immediate effects. By faith, I believe there will be long-term results as well.

Runaway emotions are our uncontrollable feelings about situations and people. They distract us from prayer. Anger, worry, and fear are runaway emotions, as are bitterness, hate, lust, doubt, and unbelief. Below are some guidelines to help you harness your emotions and let them work for you, not against you.

1. *Accept the fact that emotions arise from within you*. They are a part of your makeup. Morton Kelsey explains:

> Out of silence, disturbing emotions often come to the surface which are difficult to control. They can range from vague apprehension to terror and panic, or they may vary from bitterness and indignation to aggressive hatred and rage. Usually we attach these feelings to some object in the outer world, something we do not really need to fear, or someone who deserves our compassion rather than our anger. Most of our lives are constricted by half-conscious fears of some kind that keep us from dealing adequately with the world around us. . . . One person withdraws from being hurt because everything seems so hopeless, while another strikes back in anger at whatever seems to be causing the hurt.
>
> It is not easy to accept that these violent and disturbing emotions are a part of our being and not caused just by some situation in the outer world.[2]

2. *Face up to your emotions*. Not facing up can be dangerous. Kelsey continues:

2. Morton Kelsey, *The Other Side Of Silence* (New York, Paulist Press, 1976), p. 105.

If we deny our emotions, we do one of two things. We may successfully repress them and so cut ourselves off from one vital source of energy, becoming zombies, half dead. Or else we dam these emotions up to the point where they break loose on their own and use up that valuable energy, usually in the most destructive ways.[3]

3. *Acknowledge that positive emotions can prevent you from hearing God.* They can be as distracting as any negative emotions.

When Mary and Martha appealed to Jesus to come and heal Lazarus, they said, "Lord, behold he whom you love is sick." (John 11:3). But Jesus refused the tyranny of emotions. Having sought God's will, he stayed where he was "two days longer" before going to them in Bethany. Only then did he raise Lazarus from death. This was the greatest New Testament miracle and led to Jesus' declaration of himself as "the resurrection and the life" (v. 25).

We, too, must refuse to make hasty decisions based on emotions. Sometimes a decision creeps up on us and we are unaware that emotions have played a part in it. It can happen between friends, in families, and to a man and wife.

Johnnie and I have been married thirty-six years, and she has always had a desire to go to the Holy Land. When we received an invitation to help lead a tour of Israel, she was delighted.

But I had no real desire to go to the Holy Land — and I said so. Besides I always try to avoid travel that involves sitting on a bus all day long, looking at ruins, and spending the night in a different hotel every night. Acting on my emotions brought about two reactions. First, I avoided praying about whether or not we should go. Second, I looked for a good reason to say no.

Finally the deadline for a decision arrived. Since I was committed to the will of God, I was forced to pray about it.

The Lord directed me, "Peter, my son, you are to express your love to your wife by taking her on this trip."

I went — traveled on buses all day long, spent each night in a different hotel, looked at ruins. The whole bit. But I had a great time because I was doing the will of God rather than letting my emotions rule my life.

4. *Do not be deceived into thinking that God will automatically want the opposite of what you want.* This sadistic view about God is obviously satanically implanted.

3. Ibid.

5. *Remember, your emotions are much harder to control when you are physically down.* If possible, it is a good rule to wait to make decisions based on the will of God until you are restored in body.

6. *When you are seeking to communicate with the Lord, admit your emotions.* Do not deny them. Do not repress them. Confess exactly how you feel. Tell him your own personal preference and feelings.

7. *Ask the Lord to help you deal with your emotions.* He may have allowed them to surface just so you can present them to him to deal with. And he can transform them for his glory!

This may be difficult for you, as it is for many people. We never want to admit we feel a certain way if it doesn't seem "Christian" to us. To back off at this point because you do not like what you see and do not want to deal with it will hinder your communion with God. Push on through your feelings, knowing that he brings light into darkness and order into disorder. He will heal and change.

In *Experiencing the Depths of Jesus Christ*, Madame Jeanne Guyon writes:

> Christians have sought many ways to overcome their desires. Perhaps the most common approach has been discipline and self-denial. But no matter how severe your self-denial may be, it will never conquer your senses. . . .
>
> There is only one way to conquer your five senses,and that is by inward recollection. Or, to put it another way . . . by turning your soul completely inward to your spirit, there to possess a *present* God. . . .
>
> Your main concern lies in dwelling continually upon the God who is within you. Then, without particularly thinking of self-denial or "putting away the deeds of the flesh," God will cause you to experience a natural subduing of the flesh! . . .
>
> What, then, is required of you? All you need to do is remain steadfast in giving your utmost attention to God. He will do all things perfectly.[4]

What has been said here is that we must learn to become silent internally to properly hear from God.

The Hindrance of Wandering Thoughts

Wandering thoughts — who has not had problems with them while praying? Only the folks who have never prayed!

4. Madame Jeanne Guyon, *Experiencing the Depths of Jesus Christ* (Augusta, Maine: Christian Books, 1975), pp. 50–51.

When our thoughts jump from one thing to another during our prayer time, we show that we are unable and/or unwilling to set our minds on the Lord. This is the impediment we face when we set out to pray, only to find our minds wandering into totally unrelated subjects.

Even though we are those who are learning to bring every thought captive to the obedience of Christ, we may have unresolved conflicts that make it easy for the devil to interfere. Perhaps we have weaknesses we refuse to admit. Or we may just be physically tired and worn out.

We bring all the baggage of our past experiences to our prayer time. We have strong inner dispositions of likes and dislikes. Ideas and situations scream loudly from our inner beings and keep us from hearing God speak. The two main causes for our inattention are (1) the distracting darts of thoughts thrown by the enemy; and (2) an undisciplined mind.

The latter refers to a mind that has been habitually allowed to wander or has been "untaught" to concentrate. An article appeared in *Reader's Digest* in early 1985, suggesting that television — with its short program segments and commercial interruptions — contributes greatly to this problem. But this hindrance to one's spiritual life was as common in centuries past as it is today.

Long ago, Brother Lawrence testified of how he learned that

> ... useless thoughts spoil everything. Just there — at the point of useless thought — mischief begins!
>
> The clue — reject all useless thoughts. Reject them the moment they reveal themselves as useless to the matter at hand or to our salvation. Reject them and return to inner communion with God.[5]

Here are some practical ways of controlling your wandering thoughts:

1. *Reject thoughts that are the darts of the enemy.* As Brother Lawrence suggests, that is the first step. Reject useless thoughts for what they are: attacks of Satan.

Rejection is a definite act and differs from ignoring them. To reject these thoughts, you need to make a positive statement, such

5. Brother Lawrence, *The Practice of the Presence of God*, edited and paraphrased by Donald E. Demaray (Grand Rapids: Baker Book House, 1975), pp. 22–23.

as "Satan, get away, in the name of Jesus" or "I claim the blood of Jesus over my mind."

2. *Reject thoughts that deal with the realities of daily living.* It is often hard to reject thoughts that have to do with things that you need to remember, something very important to your routine, but Morton Kelsey gives some helpful ideas:

> It is difficult for many people to quiet their minds. As soon as they begin to center down, ideas start to come up that jar them out of the silence.... For such people it is helpful to have a notebook at hand. If one quietly records the thought ... one can let it go and return to stillness. If the thought keeps on returning, one can then push it aside and say to it: You are taken care of. Stop bothering me....
>
> Putting down in a list all the things that are flooding in upon one, without bothering about order or logic, puts them at a little distance and separates them from oneself.... Again one can speak firmly within oneself, saying to them: For right now you are taken care of. Leave me alone; I don't have to be tyrannized by you....
>
> There is a great difference between avoiding a thought or emotion and laying it aside after taking the trouble to look at it.[6]

3. *Concentrate on the indwelling Christ.* This is the most important thing in rejecting wandering thoughts. Turn inward to *him* again. The mind can only grasp one thought at a time.

This is how Madame Guyon solved the problem:

> There will be distractions, especially at the outset. And for quite some time afterward your mind will be distracted from prayer....
>
> Do *not* become distressed because your mind has wandered away. Always guard yourself from being anxious because of your faults. First of all, such distress only stirs up the soul and distracts you to outward things.
>
> Secondly, your distress really springs from a secret root of pride. What you are experiencing is in fact, a love of your own worth.
>
> How do you deal with those things that distract; how do you handle those things that draw you away from the inmost part of your being? If you should sin (or even if it is only a matter of being

6. Morton Kelsey, *The Other Side of Silence* (New York: Paulist Press, 1976), p. 110.

distracted by some circumstances around you), what should you do? *You must instantly turn within to your own spirit.*[7]

The more you are able to concentrate on Jesus, the easier it becomes to avoid the hindrance of wandering thoughts.

The Hindrance of an Empty Spiritual Life

A person with no spiritual life cannot hear God because he or she has not been born again. Such people have not had a God-encounter, although they may profess Christianity and/or been baptized. They may be "good" persons, but there have been no spiritual changes in their lives because they have not yet truly heard and accepted God's gift of grace.

Stressing the importance of this, our Lord repeated many times, "He who has ears to hear, let him hear." And you have to open both your ears and your heart before you can hear some wonderful news.

Yes, in a world filled with bad news, there is the offer of Good News — a gift from God that will bring new joy and purpose to your life. You cannot earn this gift or buy it, or be good enough to deserve it. To receive it, you must know you need it and you must want it more than anything else. It is a wonderful gift. And it is a gift no one but God can give you.

As the night sky sharpens the stars that shine, and the pain of childbirth underlines a mother's joy when she sees her newborn babe, so the darkness of bad news emphasizes the brilliance of the gospel message. To understand the Good News fully, you must know the bad news, too.

Why Do We Need Good News?

There are three reasons why we need the Good News:

Reason #1: Because of God's Character. What kind of God do you think God is? Most people have an opinion, but their opinion is not always worth much in discovering the truth. The Bible is God's way of telling us what he is like.

God declares: "I the Lord your God am holy." The apostle John says, "And this is the message we have heard from Him and an-

7. Madame Jeanne Guyon, *Experiencing the Depths of Jesus Christ* (Augusta, Maine: Christian Books, 1985), pp. 83–84.

nounce to you, that God is light, and in Him there is no darkness at all" (1 John 1:5).

God is holy. He has no evil in his character. He cannot be stained by evil; neither can he excuse evil.

Reason #2: Because God's Character Sets the Standard for Man. God created man to be like himself in character and conduct. He created human beings in his image. He created them male and female and had a divine purpose for their lives.

God planned for all his people to be the visible expression of what he, the invisible God, is like. That is God's purpose for *your* life, too, since you are one of his children.

If God were a human being, what kind of life would he live? He tells us in Exodus 20:2–17.

I am the LORD your God, who brought you out of the land of Egypt, out of the house of slavery.

You shall have no other gods before Me.

You shall not make for yourself an idol, or any likeness of what is in heaven above or on the earth beneath or in the water under the earth.

You shall not worship them or serve them; for I, the LORD your God, am a jealous God, visiting the iniquity of the fathers on the children, on the third and fourth generations of those who hate Me, but showing loving kindness to thousands, to those who love Me and keep My commandments.

You shall not take the name of the LORD your God in vain, for the Lord will not leave him unpunished who takes His name in vain.

Remember the sabbath day, to keep it holy.

Six days you shall labor and do all your work, but the seventh day is a sabbath of the LORD your God; in it you shall not do any work, you or your son or your daughter, your male or your female servant or your cattle or your sojourner who stays with you.

For in six days the LORD made the heavens and the earth, the sea and all that is in them, and rested on the seventh day; therefore the LORD blessed the sabbath day and made it holy.

Honor your father and your mother, that your days may be prolonged in the land which the LORD your God gives you.

You shall not murder.

You shall not commit adultery.

You shall not steal.

You shall not bear false witness against your neighbor.

You shall not covet your neighbor's house; you shall not covet

your neighbor's wife or his male servant or his female servant or his
ox or his donkey or anything that belongs to your neighbor.

"This is how I would live if I were a human being," says God.
"This is how I lived, when I took a human body and became man."

This kind of life — Jesus' life — reflects the high quality of God's
kind of man and woman. It is his requirement for both your outward
conduct and your inner thoughts and desires every day of your life.

*Reason #3: Because We Have Failed to Meet God's Standard of a Holy
and Righteous Life.* God is the Judge, and our good opinion of ourselves does not carry any weight with him.

God knows all things, and he says, "There is none righteous, not
even one; there is none who understands, there is none who seeks
for God; . . . for all have sinned and fall short of the glory of God"
(Rom. 3:10–11, 23).

Disobedience to God's law is called sin. When a person sins, he
breaks God's law, and sin offends Holy God.

The Judge's verdict? Guilty!

The sentence? Death! Eternal punishment and separation from
God: "For the wages of sin is death . . ."(Rom. 6:23a). "And these
[the unrighteous] will go away into eternal punishment . . ." (Matt.
25:46a).

You need the Good News because of the bad news that your
failure before God puts you in danger of eternal punishment in
hell.

What Is the Good News?

Because of love, God provided his one and only Son, Jesus Christ,
to take the punishment you deserve for not measuring up to God's
standards. Jesus Christ lived a righteous life; he never failed to obey
God's laws. He then willingly gave himself to die on a cross for your
sins. He suffered God's wrath for you. He now offers you the record
of his perfect life as a free gift.

The Bible says, "For Christ also died for sins once for all, the just
for the unjust, in order that he might bring us to God . . ." (1 Peter
3:18a). "He made Him who knew no sin to be sin on our behalf,
that we might become the righteousness of God in Him" (2 Cor.
5:21).

Christ died for your sins and mine. He offers us his righteousness.

An amazing event followed Jesus' death. Three days after his crucifixion, Jesus was declared the Son of God with power *by the resurrection from the dead*! Death was defeated, and "God has made Him both Lord and Christ" (Acts 2:36b). As Lord, he has authority to give eternal life in heaven to those who receive the Good News.

Will You Receive the Good News?

Adam, the first man, rebelled against God by disobeying God's specific command not to eat the fruit of the tree of the knowledge of good and evil. This disobedience severed his relationship with God. It brought him and all his descendants, the whole human race, into a broken relationship with God and a state of sin. Because we are born from Adam, we are born severed from God and are his enemies.

In addition, the whole human race, which came from Adam, followed in his steps of disobedience. Each has chosen to please himself rather than to obey God.

Because of God's own holiness and justice, he *must* judge man's disobedience, or sin. Yet, in love and mercy, God has provided a way out for those who will receive it.

The Bible makes it clear: "He who believes in the Son has eternal life; but he who does not obey the Son shall not see life, but the wrath of God abides on him" (John 3:36).

We either believe and obey God's Son or receive God's wrath and eternal punishment.

"What must I do?" Is that what you are asking? The Bible says, "Repent, and let each of you be baptized in the name of Jesus Christ for the forgiveness of your sins; and you shall receive the gift of the Holy Spirit (Acts 2:38).

The Holy Spirit is the Spirit of the resurrected and living Christ coming to live within you to empower you to live a new life.

To trust in someone means to count on that person to do exactly what he promised. It means you have confidence that he is able to do what he promised.

Will you trust the Lord Jesus Christ as your only means to be right with God? Will you make that commitment right now?

If, either now or in the past, you have had this kind of a God-

---

MY COMMITMENT TO JESUS

Today I receive the Good News.

I trust Jesus Christ to be my Lord and Savior—my only means to be right with God.

I commit my life to follow him daily in obedience.

Signed_____

Date_____

---

encounter, then you have spiritual life. You have been born again. You have the capacity to hear God.

The Holy Spirit
    whom Jesus also called the Spirit of Truth
    has not come into this world
    to fool around.

I would continue to oppose that kind of practice
that would take over the work of the Holy Ghost
and crowd Him out and retire Him.

This is the age of
    a superannuated Holy Ghost.
We have retired Him
    and said, "Thanks, we have our Bibles,
        good King James translation,
    and we really will not need You
        until the millennium!"

The Holy Spirit
    is still among us with transforming power
    for that one who hears the gospel message
    and really believes it.

The Spirit
    still raises the consciences of men
    out of the deep mud of their past.

He still converts.
He still regenerates.
He still transforms.
He still makes Christians out of dead clods.

It is tragic
   that we try to hide from him
      in the caves and dens of the earth,
      among the trees of the garden.

It is tragic
   that men and women keep their hearts so hard
      that they cannot feel,
   and so deaf
      that they cannot hear.[1]

1. Adapted from A. W. Tozer, *Echoes from Eden* (Harrisburg, Penn.: Christian Publications, 1981), pp. 36, 37–38.

6

The Barrier of Tradition

There is something else I would like to call to your attention that the enemy uses to block our progress on the Christian Way. It is what I call "the barrier of tradition."

For the purpose of this book, I am defining "tradition" as an inherited pattern of thought or action. Tradition is the handing down from one generation to another of information, beliefs, and customs by word of mouth or example.

Have you ever wondered about the 11:00 A.M. Sunday service? How and why it began?

The folks in farming communities found a truth in the Bible, the command to "not forsaking our own assembling together, as is the habit of some, but encouraging one another; and all the more, as you see the day drawing near" (Heb. 10:25).

Dictated by the circumstances and situations in which they found themselves, these individuals or groups — having discovered the truth — sought to give expression to it.

After morning prayer, they were led by the Holy Spirit to worship together in a certain way. In the break between the morning and afternoon chores, it was convenient for families to gather from miles around to worship God and to socialize. They thus began their services any time between nine and eleven in the morning.

And that's the way many traditions develop.

We now live in a completely different economy, but we still gather at the same time, though the cause and reasons for choosing that specific hour are no longer valid. Perhaps we need to consider a change in time or situation to meet the needs of the shift worker and other people whose schedule is unusual.

There is great blessing from God for obeying the truth in his ordained way. But it is very easy for our man-made expression of the truth to be passed on rigidly from generation to generation. Then it is often not long till the truth is forgotten and tradition is substituted for truth.

When this happens, and when God wishes us to express the truth in a new or better or more appropriate way, we cannot hear him — for we are locked into tradition.

That's the way it happened with the Pharisees. They saw a generation who had become spiritually sloppy. In their love for God, they desired to restore the command from the law of Moses: "Remember the sabbath day to keep it holy" (Exod. 20:8).

The Pharisees began to come up with ways to do this, but it was not long before their well-intentioned ideas became tradition. Their rules and regulations got longer and longer. Finally the expression of truth became more important than the truth itself.

The result was that when the Lord of the Sabbath came to give some new, higher, and better meaning to the truth, they were bound by their tradition. They rejected him and his expression of truth, which included healing a man on the Sabbath.

Truth — "not to give up meeting together" or "remember the Sabbath, to keep it holy" — is absolute. But our expressions of truth — when and how we respond — may vary according to circumstances, situations, and the leading of the Holy Spirit.

There are certain types of people who are particularly susceptible to being blocked by the barrier of tradition:

1. A *person with a godly and blessed heritage.* He has seen the blessings of God upon a past generation and may think those blessings were due to a certain way of doing things — rather than to obedience to God. Such people will not change the traditional practices that seemed to work in the past.

2. A *person who has been blessed by God in past ministry.* In the beginning a certain method was God-ordained and legitimate. Now God wants a change — a new expression of his truth. But some individuals are so set in tradition that they do not hear God's command.

Because God knows we must depend on him alone, not on a method, he will often stop blessing a procedure just so we will return to him.

3. *A person who assumes that — because a certain expression of truth (a method) worked for him — it will work for everybody.* In this case, he presses his method on others, rather than the truth itself. Thus, both discipler and disciple can become blocked by a tradition and keep the Lord out.

Traditions — familiar customs and practices and habits — are hard to discard, and many of them, with revisions dictated by God, have played an important role in preserving the elements of our faith. However, when rigidly followed, "the old ways" can become a barrier to our communication with God. There are several steps to take in averting this roadblock:

First, if you are having difficulty hearing God in a certain area, stop what you are doing! Ask the Holy Spirit to "guide you into all the truth" (John 16:13). Do not assume that you know all the answers.

Second, listen to what you are saying, since your words will help you detect where the problem might be. If you are constantly talking about a particular expression of truth, your very idea of truth could well be your trouble.

Remember what Jesus said about the Pharisees? First he quoted Isaiah the prophet: "This people honors Me with their lips, but their heart is far away from Me. But in vain do they worship Me, teaching as doctrines the precepts of men" (Mark 7:6–7, cf. Isa. 29:13). Then speaking directly to the Pharisees, he went on:

> "Neglecting the commandment of God, you hold to the tradition of men." He was also saying to them, "You nicely set aside the commandment of God in order to keep your tradition" (Mark 7:8–9).

Finally, ask yourself if you are praising God or praising a way he has ordained in the past. Be willing to change your behavior as it applies to your ways of serving our Lord. Seek his counsel about this. Begin to allow him to show you and to change all he wants to change. ". . . but they put new wine into fresh wineskins, and both are preserved" (Matt. 9:17b).

Because you want to hear God, you have first learned how to check that your equipment is in receiving order, so you may have a "hearing ear" and a "pure heart." Then you have discovered how to clear away the clutter in your life — how to avoid the traps, snares, and hindrances you may encounter on the Christian walk. The next five chapters will show you how to tune in to God's channels, how to know for sure that you are hearing him — and no other.

PART 3

Tuning In to God's Channels

God cannot violate human freedom.

He has created a race of persons
    with freedom to make choices.

He did not create fleshly robots,
    mechanical beings over which He has complete control.

He created human personalities
    made in many ways like Himself
    — in His own image
    — with a spirit akin to His own,
beings with self-consciousness
    and self-determination.
Limited, yes,
    by the kind of world we live in,
    but with enough freedom to choose
    so as to be responsible to Him. . . .

"Why doesn't God just make me good?"
But that wouldn't be goodness.
It would be slavery.

And God is not interested in slaves
but in sons and daughters!

God will not overpower us into goodness;
He can and does work through every possible means
  to get our attention,
  to call us,
  to woo us and win us.

But He will never
  ravish us or
  violate us
as persons.[1]

1. David A. Seamands, *Putting Away Childish Things* (Wheaton, Ill.: Victor Books, 1982), pp. 78–79.

7

Knowing God's Voice by His Approach

Maybe this happened to you as a child — or to your own child, more recently.... You and some friends were having a good time together when an outsider came along and wanted to join. You clammed up. You turned your back. You stopped whatever you were doing. You didn't want to have that person around, so you ignored the newcomer or even drove him away. Or you and your friends took off.

Fellowship can never be forced.

When our Lord Jesus was here on earth, he never forced himself upon people. If they didn't want him around, he left. This even happened in his own hometown, as we can read in Luke 4:16–30.

One day Jesus traveled to Nazareth, where he had grown up. And on the Sabbath day he went to the synagogue as he always had done. Jesus stood up to read and then commented on the reading.

But his fellow townsmen got very angry with what Jesus said — to the point where they forced him out of the synagogue and out of the town. They took him to the edge of a hill and wanted to throw him off, but miraculously, he walked through the crowd and went safely on his way. There is no evidence that He ever returned to Nazareth.

As in the days when he walked in the flesh, our Lord does not force his way into your life. Since he desires a relationship of love and trust, he never attempts to coerce you, though he has the ability to do so. He seeks you and offers himself to you. Whether you recognize and welcome his approach is up to you.

In What Way Does the Lord Come?

Jesus says to each one of us, "Here I am! I stand at the door and knock. If any one hears my voice and opens the door, I will come in to him, and will dine with him, and he with Me" (Rev. 3:20).

What is the door at which he knocks? In what way does the Lord come? It is through your choice to invite him in, your desire for him to come into your life. The door of the soul is the will. Jesus comes in through your choosing to "open the door."

But Jesus warns that there is another seeking entrance into your soul and another way into your life. The Lord counsels us to be alert and watchful: "Truly, truly, I say to you, he who does not enter by the door into the fold of the sheep, but climbs up some other way, he is a thief and a robber." (John 10:1). Jesus goes on to explain that the "sheep" will follow only the "shepherd," because "they know his voice" (vv. 2–4).

What does this mean? How can you distinguish the voice of the thief from the shepherd's? How can you recognize the voice of your Lord? If Jesus comes and knocks at your will, what is this "other way" the enemy uses?

Satan seeks to come in through your emotions and your reasonings. He comes appealing to your desires and to your rationality and thinking process. He bombards you with ideas and feelings, and "bombards" is a good way to identify Satan's approach!

Although the Father does speak to our sound thinking — "For God has not given us a spirit of timidity, but of power and love and discipline" (2 Tim. 1:7) — he doesn't force his way on us.

There are two things to keep in mind about God's approach:

1. *Remember that our Lord wants to come in for fellowship.* He will knock, but he will not push down the door. Just as he himself must be welcomed and wanted, his approach must be something we want. We must open the door to his presence.

2. *Remember that he who comes in by another way is a thief.* He will force his entry and then steal and rob you of all that he can.

Jesus invites us to fellowship because he understands where we are — physically, mentally, spiritually. He says, "Come to Me, all who are weary and heavy laden, and I will give you rest" (Matt. 11:28).

This is no invitation to leisure or laziness, however, for he goes on: "Take My yoke upon you, and learn from Me, for I am gentle and humble in heart; and you shall find rest for your souls." Then he gently encourages us by saying the work he asks us to do is easy. "For My yoke is easy, and My load is light" (Matt. 11:29–30).

"Since then we have a great high priest who has passed through the heavens, Jesus the Son of God, let us hold fast our confession," exults the writer to the Hebrews, possibly thinking of this invitation of Jesus. "Let us therefore draw near with confidence to the throne of grace, that we may receive mercy and may find grace to help in time of need" (Heb. 4:14, 16).

"I have loved you with an everlasting love," the Lord says through the prophet Jeremiah, "therefore I have drawn you with lovingkind-ness" (Jer. 31:3).

Think of Jesus' promises which were spoken to those who listened so eagerly two thousand years ago and are equally valid for us today:

"Ask, and it shall be given to you; seek, and you shall find; knock and it shall be opened to you. For everyone who asks receives, and he who seeks finds, and to him who knocks it shall be opened.

"Or what man is there among you, when his son shall ask him for a loaf, will give him a stone? Or if he shall ask for a fish, he will not give him a snake, will he?

"If you then, being evil, know how to give good gifts to your children, how much more shall your Father who is in heaven give what is good to those who ask Him!" (Matt. 7:7–11).

Our Lord wants you to recognize him, to know his voice by his approach. He reassures you: "But he who enters by the door is a shepherd of the sheep. To him the doorkeeper opens, and the sheep hear his voice, and he calls his own sheep by name, and leads them out" (John 10:2–4).

In this passage of Scripture, the three distinct things we are told about the approach of the Lord are (1) he comes in "through the door"; (2) he comes to lead, not drive; and (3) he is personal, not impersonal. Let us examine each of these characteristics in turn.

Our Shepherd Comes in "Through the Door"

The Lord does not force you into goodness or into anything else, but he can and does work through every possible means to get your attention. He calls. He woos. He makes himself known to you. He knocks on the door and comes in with your permission when you open the door.

Our Shepherd Leads; He Does Not Drive

Another indication that it is our Lord's voice we are hearing is in the manner of his approach. You see, the Shepherd brings all of his sheep out. Then he goes ahead of them and leads them. And they follow him because they know his voice.

This voice that leads is marked elsewhere in Scripture by such phrases as "follow me," "come after me," "go wash in the pool." In the Gospels, Jesus' call to discipleship was a call to follow, to come after. It was a call for volunteers; it was not a voice that conscripts. He calls — but you must choose whether to follow.

But there is another voice. It is the voice that drives, the voice of "the thief," the enemy. You can recognize this voice, too:

1. It *threatens* and *intimidates*, working on the basis of fear. "If you don't do this, bad things will happen."
2. It *orders*, seeking to compel by force.
3. It is *urgent* and *compulsive*. "Do it right now."

Since the relationship that the Lord desires with you is one of trust and voluntary obedience, his approach is that of a lover. There is always that aspect of invitation, of calling you. That is how you, his sheep, know your Shepherd's voice.

Our Shepherd's Approach Is Personal

In describing himself as the good shepherd, Jesus says, "He calls his own sheep, by name." Just imagine! God, the creator of all the universe, and Jesus Christ, his Son knows you by name.

But more than that, Jesus says, "I know my sheep, as the Father knows me. And my sheep know me, as I know the Father." Jesus knows everything about you, including the trivial events that make up your days.

Consider the story of how Nathanael met Jesus (John 1:45–49). Philip had found his friend under a fig tree. "... We have found Him, of whom Moses in the Law and also the Prophets wrote, Jesus of Nazareth, the son of Joseph."

"Nazareth!" The scorn dripped from Nathanael's voice. "Can anything good come from Nazareth?"

"Come and see," Philip answered.

When Jesus saw Nathanael coming toward him, he said, "Here is truly an Israelite! There is nothing false in him."

Nathanael asked, "How do you know me?"

Jesus answered, "I saw you when you were under the fig tree, before Philip called you."

Nathanael exclaimed, "Rabbi, You are the Son of God. You are the King of Israel!"

Like his approach to Nathanael, Jesus' approach to you is personal, because his relationship to you is personal.

He is the Father who approaches you as his child.

He is the Bridegroom who approaches you as his bride.

He is the Friend who approaches you as his friend.

His approach is personal because he desires fellowship. This is why John writes, "what we have seen and heard we proclaim to you also, that you also may have fellowship with us; and indeed our fellowship is with the Father and with His Son Jesus Christ" (1 John 1:3).

Fellowship is communion, communication, the interaction of lovers. Our Shepherd's call is personal. He knows each of us by name. He knows the ordinary events of our days.

But even more than that, "personal" means that you are to him a very special person. So he calls you by name. As he calls me "child," "son," "beloved son," "Peter," there is never any question in my mind as to whom he is talking.

The Shepherd has a very special relationship with you. Since he lives in you, he knows all about you. He knows about your thoughts, your feelings, your plans, your desires, your hopes, your ambitions — about all those things that only someone in an intimate personal relationship would know.

Everything he talks to us about has a personal touch to it. Sometimes when he talks to me about my wife, he says "Johnnie" and not her title, "wife." He says something like this: "Peter, Johnnie would enjoy. . . ."

Recently we were getting ready to celebrate our thirty-fifth wedding anniversary. Like many men, I am not always as thoughtful of the little things women like. As I was talking to the Lord about Johnnie, the Lord instructed me that, in appreciation for her thirty-five years of partnership, I was to have a special Love-Your-Wife Week for her. I was to give her a card and do something special for her every day for that whole week! (Among these "special things" was to give her money to spend on the grandchildren!)

It was a very special week for her — and for me — because I obeyed the Lord. We both realized in a new way that God is interested in our relationship. It turned out to be a special week for my congregation, too, as I shared with them what God had said.

Jesus' personal approach contrasts sharply with the approach of "the thief." The two approaches differ as much as the mail that comes to your home. It all has your name and address on it, but there are some important distinguishing marks between personal letters and those others — the impersonal ones that start with "Dear friend" or "Dear neighbor" or "Resident."

Even those letters that modern computers make possible, where our name is included in many places, just scream at you "form letter"! There are generalities about them that we recognize. Missing is that intangible element that only a personal relationship makes possible.

Approaches by telephone differ, too. Though an anonymous caller may use a warm, friendly approach like an old friend, it doesn't take you long to realize it's not a personal call. In the same way, the approach of the enemy has about it an impersonal nature that can be detected, even though he seeks to imitate the personal approach of the Lord Jesus.

Our Lord's approach to you is so personal that you recognize him. You know by his approach that it is the Lord!

I *was regretting the past,*
 fearing the future.

Then . . . *suddenly . . .*
my Lord *was speaking.*

My *name is*
I AM

　　He *paused.*
　　I *waited.*
　　He *continued.*

When *you live in the past*
 with its mistakes and regrets
it *is hard.*

I AM
not there.
My *name is not*
I WAS.

When *you live in the future*
 with its problems and fears
it *is hard.*

I AM
not there.
My *name is not*
I WILL BE.

When you live in this moment,
it is not hard.

I AM
here.
My name is
I AM.

Helen Mallicoate

8

Knowing God's Voice by His Relevance

As I write this I am on vacation in Jackson Hole, Wyoming. It is a very special vacation and was given to me by God through the church. It is special as the first time in thirty-five years of marriage that my wife and I have had two weeks together alone, away from the responsibilities of ministry. It is special because my body, soul, and spirit needed refreshment. It was given to us to rest.

However, there are many burdens that I carry for members of my family and for the church and many of its members. It would be very natural for my time here to be filled with thoughts about matters that I can do absolutely nothing about. But I have come to see that other than to pray, such thoughts are not from the Lord.

My Lord is a relevant God, and he wants to walk with me *now* and *here* — not as my mind struggles with concerns two thousand miles away and weeks into the future.

In these days I have recognized his voice as he has spoken to me about where I am today. Because he is a relevant God, I can expect his message to be relevant. (Praise him, they have been!)

By way of example, as we have toured through two great national parks, Grand Teton and Yellowstone, the Lord has spoken to me of how he is a "refuge," and — just as animals come and live protected from harm in these parklands — I will experience the same if I come to live in union and fellowship with him. With this and so much more, he has refreshed my soul, providing relief from worries and concerns.

God's voice always has relevance, meaning that it has to do with the matter at hand, that it is pertinent and applicable. Our God is a God of the here and now. His voice is relevant in regard to *time, resources, circumstances, comprehension*, as he speaks to us in his self-established ways.

Knowing God's Voice by His Relevance to Time

Do you live in the "here and now"?

Jesus emphasized *today*: "So do not be anxious for tomorrow; for tomorrow will care for itself. Each day has enough trouble of its own" (Matt. 6:34).

Our Lord Jesus indicates here that his communications are always timely. He, who commands you not to be concerned about tomorrow, will not burden your mind with concern about the future. When your thoughts are filled with worries and cares about what tomorrow may bring, you can be sure you are not hearing his voice. Jesus commands you to be concerned about today, and he will certainly guide you about the present.

Of course, the most fundamental reasons for discarding your future-oriented concerns are God's abiding presence and his desire to have continual fellowship with you. So important is this to him, and so earnest is his desire that you be reassured, that he has promised, "I will never desert you, nor will I ever forsake you" (Heb. 13:5b).

Our Lord knows that the most important period of time is always "the now." He knows that your "nows" will soon become your yesterdays and that if you live each "now" well, you will have no regrets. He also knows that your "nows" determine your future and that when the future becomes "now," it will be good if you have lived each past moment well.

"The now" — the precious present — is quite obviously the secret to a full life. How often we focus on the big events of the future — a family Christmas celebration, the coming conference, Father's Day, a high-school graduation. But God wants each of us, you and me, to focus on what is happening *today*, and the relevance of the Lord's voice regarding time is one of the ways to know the Shepherd's voice. His focus is always on "the now."

In contrast, the enemy tries to divert your attention to the past or the future. He knows that anyone who looks back on the path of life will trip and stumble. He also knows that a person who is concentrating on tomorrow is living in an illusion that prevents him from living fully now.

God does give goals and promises for the future, but, remember, his focus is on the present!

TRUTH: He is God of "The Now."

Knowing God's Voice by His Relevance to Resources

While attending seminary in 1955, I was involved in a car accident. There was a $100-deductible clause in my insurance policy. That was a lot of money — far more than I could possibly foresee paying. My wife and I contemplated my dropping out of seminary and going to work full time. But we decided to pray about it.

I will never forget that Saturday morning as we knelt at our dining room table and committed our problem to the Lord. He said to us as plainly as could be, "I brought you here to go to seminary and not to take another job. Continue. I will provide."

Within an hour a letter arrived for us in which there was a cashier's check for $100 from a town in Texas that I had never heard of before. You can imagine how joyously a 24-year-old preacher praised the Lord that day!

I was beginning to learn that God's voice is always relevant in regard to resources — ours and his. God's message for you is always conditioned on his knowledge of the resources that are available to you, from *his* viewpoint and not from yours.

He would not have you worry about seemingly inadequate resources, even those as fundamental as your basic needs for food and clothing. For those walking with him, God promises to supply all our needs. ". . . do not be anxious for your life, as to what you shall eat, or what you shall drink; nor for your body, as to what you shall put on. Is not life more than food, and the body than clothing?" (Matt. 6:25).

Then, pointing to the birds flying around, Jesus adds: ". . . they do not sow, neither do they reap, nor gather into barns, and yet your heavenly Father feeds them." A slight pause and he continues, "Are you not worth much more than they?" (v. 26).

The people listening to Jesus then were as worried about life's necessities as we are today. And so he asked, "And which of you by being anxious can add a single cubit to his life's span?" Then he pointed to the *source* of food and clothes and of life itself: . . . "for your heavenly Father knows that you need all these things" (Matt. 6:27, 32).

My seminary experience, and many other experiences God has walked me through, clearly show that "the God who guides, provides." So does Jesus' miracle in the Matthew 14:13–21 account:

Jesus wanted to get away by himself (like any one of us might), after the murder of his cousin John the Baptist. So he took a boat to escape to a lonely place. But the people heard about it, followed him by land, and were waiting for him when he landed.

It was a long day for Jesus, healing the sick and teaching. As the evening shadows lengthened, the disciples began wondering what to do with the large crowd.

They tried to solve this problem in much the same way you and I would: "Let's give the responsibility to another agency. We don't have the budget or manpower for this new demand." That's what they meant when they asked Jesus to send the people away and let them fend for themselves.

But that was not then — nor is it now — Jesus' way. He had other plans: ". . . 'They do not need to go away; you give them something to eat' " (v. 16).

It is easy to understand where these fellows were in their thinking. I've done this over and over again. Possibly you have, too. I tell God what the problem is — and then, when he gives the solution, I explain to him why his idea will never work.

And that's the way the disciples reacted to the needs of the crowd. Looking at their meager supplies, they give Jesus a reasonable assessment of the limitations of their resources: "We've been able to get together only five loaves and two fish" (v. 17).

They, like us, forgot that the God who leads, feeds. He supplies the resources.

How different God wants it to be! When you come up against a need you cannot meet, that should become the stimulus that turns your attention to the Supplier. He has promised never to fail you nor forsake you and to supply all your needs according to his riches.

Jesus understood the disciples' problem. He knew their resources. He saw that they were overwhelmed and frustrated before the enormity of the need. And he simply said, "Bring them here to Me" (v. 18). Jesus did not ask his disciples to do anything for which he did not already have adequate resources provided.

It is so for you and me today. From our perspective we see shortages and no resources. But the supply from God's perspective is always there *before* the need is created.

What about your time? That's one of your most important resources. Maybe you feel like the disciples — facing shortages, with no reserves. Our Lord's communication with you in regard to your time is the same as it was then. He deals with what resources you have, not with what you do not have.

Jesus does not ask you to give time you do not have. He asks for whatever time you *do* have. Just like he broke the five loaves and two fish, he can do more with the ten minutes you give to him than with ten hours you do not have. Sometimes he chooses to have you use those ten minutes in ministry to another person by phone, letter, or a conversation across the fence.

Jesus knows *all* your resources — time and money — before he asks for them. And, when you give them to him, then our Lord uses them for his glory. He speaks to you about what is needed now to carry out his will for the present. He does not usually speak to you about your anticipated or imagined need for a future ministry in the tomorrows.

That is why James, inspired by the Holy Spirit, strongly and practically admonishes, "Come now, you who say, 'Today or tomorrow, we shall go to such and such a city, and spend a year there and engage in business and make a profit.' Yet you do not know what your life will be like tomorrow" (James 4:13–14a).

That is God's way! He wants us to trust him to use what we already have in order to provide whatever is needed to do his work.

In contrast, the enemy will focus on such things as the meagerness of our resources. He whispers, "You have so little to give. Why bother?" Satan stresses our imagined lacks and anticipated needs. He reinforces our fear of not having enough in the future, of being a burden on our children or others. "Where are you going to get what you need tomorrow?" he jeers.

TRUTH: The God who guides, provides — on time!

Knowing God's Voice by His Relevance to Circumstances

"If I did not have these circumstances, I would. . . ."
How many times such thoughts have flooded through my mind!
Let me share a few with you:

> "If I did not have to deal with church administration, how much more I could do for God!"

> "If I did not have to cut our grass, if my wife did not have to cook and clean, how much more could my wife and I do for the Lord!"

> "If I did not have to work with people who seem to be unco-operative, indifferent to the Lord's will, what great things could happen to the church for God's glory!"

Such thinking is not from God. For he not only knows my cir-cumstances, but — even if he did not cause them — he certainly has allowed them. God knows our present circumstances and will cause us to be most triumphant and valuable where we are. But if we are upset or waiting for circumstances to change, we will neither hear him where we are nor accomplish very much.

Would John Bunyan have been able to write the classic *Pilgrim's Progress* if he had been wishing for other circumstances? No. God saw him where he was, in jail for his beliefs, and used him there.

Imagine what would have happened if Paul had fought his cir-cumstances. What if he had spent his time daydreaming about what might have been if he were "free." Suppose Paul had said, "If I were out of jail, I could start more churches!" Suppose his thoughts were always along this line of thinking: he would have missed God's will. And there are many precious words of the Bible we would never have received, since some of his Epistles were written from prison. Think of what we would have missed!

Our Lord's communication with us will be about our *present* cir-cumstances, which he alone knows completely. He is always with us, and he either created or allowed our circumstances. He does not speak to us about what could be if such and such were the situation. He speaks about what can be as things are now.

What are your circumstances? Do you have small children at home? Are you trying to be both mother and father to your children? Do you have an anti-God husband or wife? Are you in a half-dead church? Do you have a mean boss? Are you living in a bad neighborhood?

God knows these things, and he will speak to you about what is happening now — not what might be "if." He will tell you how — in *your* circumstances — you can let your light shine for his glory.

The enemy will try to get you to focus on the wrong interpretation of your situation. He would have had Paul say, "I am a prisoner of Rome," as if that ended his usefulness. Satan wants you to see the limitations of your circumstances, rather than the opportunities.

If Paul had concentrated on the prison guard as an enemy — if Paul had not recognized the real enemy — then the description of Christian armor would never have been written.

TRUTH: The Lord speaks to you in the midst of your circumstances.

Knowing God's Voice by His Relevance to Your Comprehension

My wife and I communicate on a far different level now, after thirty-five years of marriage, than we did when we first began our life together. We understand and love each other so deeply that one word may communicate a dozen sentences, one glance may carry a full message.

Here are a few examples:

My wife has a certain way of looking at the dining table. It is just a hundredth-of-a-second glance that says to me and other members of the family: "There is not enough food for all the guests who have dropped in. Family, go easy on your portions. You can get some more after the meal is over. Please don't take more than one slice of meat."

My wife has another look that says, "Do not say any more. This is a time to keep quiet. If you say any more, you will regret it. Please keep quiet!"

My wife also has a twist of her head that says, "I can handle this situation. Please stay out of it. It will be better for now if I do it myself."

I could go on and on. She communicates with me now in a way and on a level that I can understand but nobody else would be able to fully grasp. Likewise, I'm sure there are words and gestures of mine that are meaningful only to her.

Like a mother who communicates with her child on the child's level, so the Lord knows where you are and what you understand. And it is in just that place that he communicates with you.

Our Lord treated his disciples in the same way. He understood where they were in their journey of faith. At one time, Jesus told them, "I have many more things to say to you, but you cannot bear them now" (John 16:12).

Jesus treats you today the same way. Knowing what you can "bear," he gently leads you into more light, into greater understanding of his ways.

Your comprehension is so important to God that he made a covenant about it! "I'll make this agreement with the people of Israel," he said. "I will put My law within them, and on their heart I will write it; and I will be their God, and they shall be my people" (Jer. 31:33).

As a first-grader learns phonetics, then progresses on to simple words, and soon is reading books, so you must learn God's truth step by step.

David had this kind of Father-child relationship with God. "O Lord, my heart is not proud," he wrote, revealing the confidence of a child in his loving, all-knowing Father, "or my eyes haughty; nor do I involve myself in great matters, or in things too difficult for me. Surely, I have composed and quieted my soul; like a weaned child rests against his mother, my soul is like a weaned child within me" (Ps. 131:1–2).

Is this your attitude when situations and problems arise that are too much for you?

". . . God is light and in him there is no darkness at all" (1 John 1:5). God will communicate with you on a level you can grasp and understand. He will speak to you plainly about that which is clear and understandable to you.

TRUTH: God speaks plainly — confusion and misunderstanding are not from him.

Knowing God's Voice by His Relevance in Regard to His Self-Established Ways

One of the hard things I have had to learn since God gave me a wife to complete me is that he intended to complete me in that particular way and with that particular person.

I would rather he speak directly to me, although sometimes I don't listen. And sometimes he decides not to be boxed in by some former way of working (speaking directly to me) and chooses another of his self-established ways.

I often am inclined to spend a week and pay a thousand dollars to hear some national speaker and teacher tell me a truth that God would have used my wife to tell me for free and in five minutes. How foolish can we be?

I believe I am a very fast thinker. I have prided myself in this ability to think something through quickly and give a bottom-line conclusion. But sometimes I am a slow responder!

For years my wife (and the Lord through my wife) has begged me to slow down and to spell out to her not only the bottom line, but how I got there. I have not listened to her and as a result have hurt my ministry at home and in the church. God is finally getting through to me by this ordained and planned channel: my wife.

God uses all and any of the channels and ways he has established. God's answer to you will be related to the ways he himself set up. You can expect him to operate in the way he has already laid out.

David Seamands refers to C. S. Lewis, who pointed out in *God in the Dock* that

> God works miracles, not magic, for no one makes bread out of stones — not even God. He turns seeds into wheat or corn or rye and out of that we make bread. When Jesus fed the Five Thousand, He didn't take stones from the brook and turn them into bread and fish. He took loaves and made more loaves, fish and multiplied them into more fish. And this is what farmers do every year and the fish do in season — produce more bread and more fish. It takes them a long

time to do it through the laws of nature. But Jesus Christ, being the Lord of both time and nature, can speed up the process into a few minutes.[1]

For some things, however, God does not take short cuts. There was no "short cut" for Jesus to becoming King of kings and Lord of lords, because that was God's will.

In the temptation in the desert (Matt. 4:1–11), when Satan suggested that Jesus do "magic" and make bread from stones, he also asked Jesus to jump from the top of the temple. *But Jesus refused to violate the law of gravity in order to create a sensation.*

When the devil suggested that Jesus turn stones into bread (Matt. 4:3), it was more than a mere temptation to take a short cut to popularity. It was a typically devilish suggestion, for Satan is essentially a magician.

All this in no way means that God is a prisoner of his own universe. God can intervene with higher laws that we know nothing about. An airplane does not break the law of gravity when it flies; it supersedes it with a higher law — the law of aerodynamics.

Our God is supernaturally natural — that is to say, his supernaturalness works through natural things that he created. His ways are the ways he himself set up: the natural methods, the natural authorities, the natural laws.

The enemy concentrates on magic, on sensationalism and short cuts that seem to violate God's laws.

David Seamands explains:

> God made this world to operate according to certain laws. We don't know all those laws; we've been a long time discovering some of them and we've got many more to go. These laws really come out of the character of God Himself and express His inner stability and reliability....
>
> Much disillusionment with prayer is caused by childish misunderstanding of how God works in relationship to this world.
>
> Let me use an extreme illustration. Let us say there is a married couple who, though they desire a child very much, have so far not been able to have one. They could pray in several different ways which would in every case involve either that they would be able to

---

1. David A. Seamands, *Putting Away Childish Things* (Wheaton, Ill.: Victor Books, 1982), p. 78.

have a baby or that God would enable them to adopt a child. We can't imagine any couple who would pray for God to somehow drop a baby into their laps from heaven. But why not? Can't God do anything? It's not hard to see the foolishness and falseness in this kind of reasoning.[2]

TRUTH: God, the Creator, works according to his own established ways.

We can know it is God's voice speaking to us because his voice is relevant. Relevant in regard to *time*. Relevant in regard to *resources*. Relevant in regard to *circumstances* and relevant in regard to our *comprehension*. And God's voice is always speaking to us in his self-established ways.

2. Ibid., p. 77.

There was a voice from the firmament
that was over their heads
when they stood
and had let down their wings.

Ezekiel 1:25

One night I was much troubled by anxious thoughts;
they came beating on me through those hours,
    and I could not get away from them;
    I could hear no reassuring voice.

At last I remembered Ezekiel 1,
    which I had read the day before,
and I began to see that
        the wings of the will
        and the wings of the work
were not the only wings that must be let down.

There were others,
    there were the wings of anxious thoughts.

Those wings were not easy to let down.
But when at last they were down
    this was the word:

"Hast thou not known?
Hast thou not heard
    that the everlasting God
    the Lord
    the Creator of the ends of the earth
fainteth not,
    neither is weary? . . .

He giveth power to the faint;
and to them that have no might
He increaseth strength." [1]

9

Knowing God's Voice
by Its Content (1)

Suppose ten different people were to phone you, all claiming to be your spouse. Even if all had exactly the same voice accent and pattern, it would not be difficult to tell which one was really your wife or husband, would it?

A man would know his wife on the basis of content of the con-
versation. Out of his relationship with her would come certain statements and facts that none of the other women would be able to make.

One's wife could ask and answer questions that none of the others could. She would make statements about previous situations that you both knew about. Facts would be stated that would be relevant because of common knowledge. She would use vocabulary that was distinctly hers. A man would soon know she was his wife, and a woman would be able to recognize her husband's voice in the same way.

Similarly, the conversation your Lord would have with you is one that comes out of a relationship of fellowship together. Certain aspects of content would reveal who was speaking.

Do you know what God would talk to you about? There are at least seven recognizable topics, and you know God's voice by the content of what he says (1) about himself; (2) about himself in reference to Scripture; (3) about situations where guidance is given; (4) about sin; (5) about yourself; (6) about relating to others; and (7) about faith.

God, in communicating with you, will spend much time on subjects that are of vital importance to him and to you. His desire is to have fellowship with you, to love you and for you to love him. When the Lord communicates with you, he will deal with matters that will enable his desires to take place in you in an ever-increasing way.

Knowing God's Voice by What He Says About Himself

Religion — any and all religions — are nothing more than man's response to the God he knows or thinks he knows. A wrong concept of God will bring a wrong response.

The Auca headhunters of the Amazon jungle believe that, because God is good, he can be ignored and his "goodness" will continue. However, because Satan is evil, they have to continually do all they can to placate him. Trying to get Satan to leave them alone, they practice superstitious and even murderous acts.

Civilized man is generally afraid of God. This fear results in a wrong kind of relationship. God, by revelation of himself, seeks to eliminate the fear.

Throughout the Bible, God seeks man. God makes provisions so that man may approach him for fellowship. God makes himself known so there can be the proper relationship.

God wants to make himself known to *you*. He wants you to listen carefully when he speaks to you about himself so that you may know him as he really is. Because of all this, you can expect God to reveal himself in his conversation.

Holy God as Father

Jesus came to show you what God is really like. He showed you this by what he did and by what he taught. By behaving toward God as a son to his father, Jesus taught men that God was Father — the highest revelation of God. God is above and before all else your Father. This is what he is to you.

A holy Father. A perfect Father. A loving Father. A merciful Father. A good Father. A righteous Father. A heavenly Father.

In the New Testament, the word *Father* is used to refer to God 267 times. The only New Testament book that does not refer to him in this way is 3 John. The Epistles are written on the basis that God is Father.

The Voice of Our Father

In God's self-revelation to you, you can know him by the underlying concept that he speaks as the Father who has chosen you, begotten you as his child, and plans to fulfill the responsibilities of his fatherhood to you.

The enemy is very subtle at this point. He likes to take an aspect of God and either magnify it out of all proportion or minimize it as not important at all. For example, with one person Satan might so magnify the holiness of God that a basic fear of God makes that person fearful of almost everything. At the same time, the enemy is minimizing God's love.

With someone else, this "thief" might do exactly the opposite. He could overemphasize the love of God, saying, "God loves you so much that he will never chastise you. You can sin all you want and God will not really care." When this is the case, holiness is minimized. Out of this caricature of God will come another set of reactions. total self centeredness and self-indulgence, leading ul*timately to depression and death.

The content of any word from God about himself begins with the basic fact that he is our Father. With his Father-child relationship at the center, all else can have its proper place.

Knowing God's Voice by How Its Content Relates to Scripture

More than any other source, your meditation should come out of the Scriptures. When our Lord is applying the Scriptures to you, he never violates their principles.

However, the enemy tries to move in to interpret the Scriptures. He uses isolated fragments of Scripture with you, just as he did with Jesus in the desert temptation (Matt. 4:1–11).

Satan led Jesus to Jerusalem, remember? And put him on a high place of the temple. Then he said to Jesus, "If You are the Son of God throw yourself down; for it is written, 'He will give His angels charge concerning You'; and 'On *their* hands they will bear You up, lest You strike Your foot against a stone' " (v. 6).

Jesus answered, "On the other hand, it is written, 'You shall not put the LORD your God to the test' " (v. 7).

The enemy tempted our Lord to act in an unbecoming way, using fragments of two Old Testament verses as "prooftexts." Jesus, aware of the trap because of his true knowledge of all Scripture, replied with a basic principle of God.

Do you know the difference between a prooftext and a divine principle? A prooftext is often a statement lifted out of its context to prove a particular viewpoint. This is the technique Satan used in Jesus' temptation. Jesus, however, replied with a basic principle of God. This principle is a divine way of operating that comes out of the character and power of God.

How can you know if you are interpreting Scripture correctly? You can know that the content of the Lord's message will never violate the principles, the great underlying truths, that are consistently spelled out in Scripture.

James carefully details one of these principles when he writes, "The wisdom from above is first pure, then peaceable, gentle, reasonable, full of mercy and good fruits, unwavering, without hypocrisy" (3:17).

It is never right to do wrong in order to do right. The end never justifies the means.

Let's look at some practical examples of the outworking of that principle:

1. It is not right to steal in order to help the poor.
2. It is not right to stop work on the job you are paid to do so you can pray — unless you are paid to pray.
3. It is not right to lie to keep from hurting someone's feelings.
4. It is not right to neglect our worship of God for his work (service).

The more zealous you are to do the work of God, the easier it is to fall prey to Satan's manipulative use of prooftexts. Knowing the principles of the Word and knowing that the Holy Spirit will not lead us to violate them is of vital importance in listening to God's voice.

Knowing God's Voice by How the Content Relates to His Guidance

How can you tell if the guidance about a direction of life, a problem to be solved, or a decision to be made comes from God?

James helps us out with this question: "If any of you lacks wisdom, let him ask of God, who gives to all men generously and without reproach, and it will be given to him. But let him ask in faith without any doubting, for the one who doubts is like the surf of the sea driven and tossed by the wind. For let not that man expect that he will receive anything from the Lord" (1:5–7).

Three basic principles about the way God works can help you.

1. *God is more interested in the development of your character than he is in changing your circumstances.* God's committal to us centers around conformity to Christ. God is not interested in helping us develop a philosophy of escape from problems by more dependence on him. He wants us to have a philosophy of triumph in overcoming problems.

Therefore, you can expect that God's wisdom to you will deal more with the development of your character than with circumstances. He knows that when Christ is in charge in you, the circumstances will change you. He may or may not change the circumstance.

Are you asking God to give you a new job because of adverse conditions where you are at present? Often it is not his will to change your circumstances. He uses those circumstances to transform you!

Like me, most people asking God for a change in their family situation are seeking guidance in how to help the other member(s) of the family change. I, for example, earnestly prayed for a change in my son, Richard, when he was involved in drugs. But God usually works first in the "pray-er," the person doing the praying. God dealt with me about my pride before he ever answered my prayer and touched Richard.

Before he changes the others involved, God's solution will be to show you how *you* can become more like Christ. Being a better father or mother, more like Christ, automatically means a better home. So, from my own experience, my advice to dads and moms who come to me for help is to "see what God is saying to you and what he wants to do in you."

The content of God's speaking to you will usually include those things that will develop your character, rather than change your circumstances.

2. *God deals with attitudes and concepts more than he deals with behavior.* God knows that problems are often caused by our inner condition, so he usually has an inner solution rather than an outer one.

The enemy, too, knows that behavior is symptomatic of the soul's condition. He knows that a hypocrite is a person whose inner and outer life are not in harmony. He therefore works to encourage us to an outer change of behavior rather than an inner change of mind, emotions, or will.

Is the cup of your life filled with sweet living water? Then, no matter how you are jostled or pushed, only sweet living water will spill out. Is there bitter envy, selfish ambition, disorder, and evil practices in your life? That bitter water will spill out when you are upset by your circumstances.

Jesus knew how easily this happens to any of us. On one occasion, he said to the Pharisees and teachers of the law, "Rightly did Isaiah prophesy of you hypocrites, as it is written, 'This people honors Me with their lips, but their heart is far away from Me. But in vain do they worship Me, teaching as doctrines the precepts of men'" (Mark 7:6–7).

The devil does not mind if you go to church and perform other acts of religious devotion, as long as there is no real devotion in your heart. He knows that a person cannot pretend all the time. The real condition of your heart will show in loose moments and cause discredit to God's name.

Our Lord examines your heart to bring about changes there. Therefore, he usually has an inner solution rather than an outer one. Jesus is aiming for a change in heart. That's why he told us: "You have heard that the ancients were told, 'You shall not commit murder' and 'Whoever commits murder shall be liable to the court'" (Matt. 5:21).

Then and now we would all agree with that!

He continued, "But I say to you that everyone who is angry with his brother shall be guilty before the court ...". (v. 22). This was different. This was hitting home where most of us live. This was "getting personal." And we don't like that!

Jesus knew this and gave the solution: "If therefore you are presenting your offering at the altar, and there remember that your brother has something against you, leave your offering there before the altar, and go your way; first be reconciled to your brother, and then come and present your offering" (vv. 23–24).

3. *The Lord guides you with "Yes" or "No."* The Lord does not tell you to do what he himself would not do. God means what he says, and he will give you a "Yes" or "No" answer. You are to be like him, so he commands you: "Let your yes be yes, and your no, no" (James 5:12b). If you must say more than "yes" or "no," it is from the enemy.

Imagine the pastor of your church next Sunday morning asking all the members to consider giving up three hours one afternoon to a special ministry to the poor. Both your heavenly Father and the devil would be glad to tell you what to do.

The enemy's approach through your mind would usually be either of the following:

1. Motivation to do it: thoughts of guilt and accusation. "You are not doing your share." Or "You need to do something because you are not paying your employees properly at the plant."
2. Motivation *not* to do it: thoughts of rationalism and defense. "You should not take time from your family." Or "You volunteered last time." Or "You are not good at that."

The Father's approach in giving wisdom for such a situation would be different. When you asked him what to do, he would say "Yes, this is my will for you" or "No, this is not my will for you." Our Father guides us, leads us, tells us what to do — rather than reasoning with us. Just as you make decisions for your small child because the child cannot understand all the ins and outs, so God knows you cannot understand all the "whys" of a matter.

None of us is capable of thinking like God does. His ways and his thoughts are as far above ours as the heavens are above the earth.

But you can trust him. You can obey him. This is what walking in the Holy Spirit is. You do or you do not do things because of obedience and trust, *not* because of guilt and reasonings.

4. *"The fear of the* LORD *is the beginning of wisdom . . ."* (Ps. 111:10). Guidance is a necessary part of the content of God's message to

you, since you have never before been this way on the road of life, and an enemy is seeking to entrap you.

Guidance is also a promise of God to you. Both the Old and New Testaments arc full of such promises for you. The Lord says, "I will instruct you and teach you in the way which you should go; I will counsel you with My eye upon you" (Ps. 32:8).

Talking about the Holy Spirit whom he was going to send, Jesus promised, "But when He, the Spirit of truth, comes, He will guide you into all the truth; for He will not speak on His own initiative, but whatever He hears, He will speak; and He will disclose to you what is to come. He shall glorify Me; for He shall take of Mine, and shall disclose it to you" (John 16:13–14).

Remember what we have discussed in previous chapters: God is not boxed in by a single method, a certain way, a unique means, an established procedure. There are many ways and many vehicles the Holy Spirit uses to guide us into all truth. Most often, he uses the Scriptures. Sometimes he uses human authorities in their particular area. Sometimes he uses a family member, either a flesh relative or a spiritual brother or sister. Sometimes a specific situation is used to lead us to truth.

In fact, God's Spirit can and does use a diverse number of vehicles to speak to us. But, whatever his methods, we need to be able to discern his voice so that Satan will not be able to get at us through perverting these means.

The secret is knowing what God is talking about!

Jesus recognized Satan when he was speaking through Simon Peter — and rebuked him for it. This was the same Peter who a few moments before had uttered words of highest revelation that Jesus said had come from God. Jesus was able to recognize the Father and Satan in the same human being because he knew the Father's voice. And that is what he wants for us, too.

In this chapter we have discussed three ways in which the content of the message can help us recognize God's voice talking to us: knowing God's voice by what he says about himself, by what he says in reference to Scriptures, by what he says in giving guidance. In the next chapter we will look at four other ways we can recognize God's voice by paying attention to the subject matter of his words.

When I was a little child
   I used to wish I could touch something
      our Lord Jesus touched, or see something He saw.

Then suddenly to my delight I thought,
   but I can see something that He saw.

He saw the very same moon and stars that I see.

And I used to look at the moon
   and think, He saw you,
He saw those funny marks in your face. . . .
He looked up to you just as I look up to you tonight.

Years afterward someone gave me a bit of brick
   and a little slab of marble from Rome.
It was wonderful to touch one of them and think,
   perhaps the apostle Paul or one of the martyrs
   touched this as they passed.

But how much more wonderful is it to think
   that we have, for our own use,
   the very same sword our Lord used
   when the devil attacked Him.

Let us learn "the word of God,"
  that these "definite utterances of God"
  may be ready in our minds;
    ready for use at the moment of need —
our sword which never grows dull and rusty,
  but is always keen and bright. . . .

Let us not expect defeat
  but victory.

Let us take fast hold
  and keep fast hold
of our sword,
and we shall win in any assault of the enemy.[1]

---

1. Adapted from Amy Carmichael, *Edges of His Ways* (Fort Washington, Penn.: Christian Literature Crusade [S.P.C.K., 1955]), pp. 39–40.

10

Knowing God's Voice by Its Content (2)

Have you ever felt guilty and yet could not find a sin to confess? Then, believing you were under a dark cloud of guilt, you probably ended up praying something like this: "Dear Lord, forgive me for the things I have done that I should not have done and for the things I left undone and all other bad things."

I have done that — more times than I would like to admit. In shame I say it, because this type of prayer is not motivated by the Lord Jesus, but by the Evil One who is the accuser and enemy of the brethren. Such a prayer is a direct response to the condemnation of the Evil One, because one of the ways the enemy gets at us is by false guilt.

Since false guilt and real guilt feel exactly the same, how can we tell the difference? How do we know God's voice in this important matter of sin? Taking this a bit further, what does God tell us about ourselves, our relationships, and our faith?

Knowing God's Voice by How the Content Relates to Our Sins

One of the segments in Jesus' promise of the Holy Spirit has to do directly with sin. The Holy Spirit "will convict the world concerning sin, and righteousness, and judgment; concerning sin, because they do not believe in Me" (John 16:8–9).

If the Holy Spirit dwells in you, directing and controlling you, that promise will be fulfilled. He *will* convict you of sin, thereby assuring you that you belong to God.

It is inevitable that any loving father will have to deal with the behavior of his children when they do wrong. God the father deals with your behavior as his child for many reasons. First, sin hurts you and it hurts other people; so he chastises you because he loves you. Second, God is holy and righteous; so he cannot tolerate sin, which is discordant with his nature and offends him. Third, sin blocks his ever-increasing fellowship with you.

All Scripture and the experience of all the saints of the ages testify that God takes action *directly* and *personally* with sinners. Since Satan always attacks and attempts to corrupt what God is doing, it is not surprising that he will try to corrupt genuine conviction, perverting it with an imitation conviction, which is called "condemnation."

Since conviction and condemnation are very much alike, many sincere Christians suffering from condemnation think they are under conviction. The following outline may help you tell the difference:

Conviction by the Holy Spirit	**Condemnation by the Enemy**
1. *Definite and specific.* The Lord tells me exactly what I have done.	1. *Indefinite and vague.* I feel guilty but cannot identify any specific sin.
2. *Recognizable.* It is something unconfessed and unforgiven that I recognize — usually in the immediate past.	2. *Imaginary.* I have a hard time putting my finger on this — unless it is something in the past that I have already taken care of.
3. *Definite solution.* The Holy Spirit tells me how to take care of the sin. When I obey, I get relief from soul-pain guilt.	3. *Usually no solution.* If any solution is offered, it is irrational and unscriptural. The soul-pain intensifies.

Your loving Father will tell you, his child, what you have done and how you must correct it. This is genuine conviction.

Knowing God's Voice by How the Content Relates to Our Self-Image

For a good part of my Christian life I have been crippled by a bad spiritual Self-image. Thoughts would sometimes come into my mind such as, "I am no good." "I will never amount to anything." "I am a failure." "I am a nobody." These thoughts that I had accepted had often driven me to despair — that is, until I found that they came from the enemy.

A proper God-image and a proper self-image are indispensable to the Christian life. If either of these is crippled, your spiritual walk will be halting and lame. The Lord therefore seeks to build to maturity both your God-image and your self-image.

When people care deeply for each other, they express how they feel about each other. The Lord will often talk to you about how he feels about you. No one who listens to him talk this way will ever have a bad self-image or come away discouraged. *Your self-worth is never attacked by the Lord.* Do you know you are extremely valuable to the Lord? Just think:

> *When Project Earth is over —*
> the creation,
> the coming of Jesus,
> the coming of the Holy Spirit,
> plus all the other things our God has done in
> his involvement on earth —
> *do you know all he is going to get from it?*
> Not silver and gold.
> Not art.
> Not buildings.
> Not literature.
> *Jesus is going to get just one thing:*
> PEOPLE — LIKE YOU AND ME.

All God has ever done, he did to have a family, a bride, a living temple. You are one of his children. You are his project. You are valuable, precious, special to him. So special, in fact, that God had one of his servants offer encouragement to you! Paul writes:

> I pray that the eyes of your heart may be enlightened, so that you may know what is the hope of His calling, what are the riches of the glory of His inheritance in the saints, and what is the surpassing greatness of His power toward us who believe. These are in accordance with the working of the strength of His might which He brought

about in Christ, when He raised Him from the dead, and seated Him at His right hand in the heavenly places (Eph. 1:18–20).

Any mental attack on your self-worth does not come from the Father. He will correct your behavior, but he never condemns your worth.

It is the enemy who sends all such thoughts as "I am no good." "I will never amount to anything." "I am a failure." "I am a nobody." "I am not important."

But God says we are his "inheritance" (Eph. 1:18) and his "saints" (1 Cor. 1:2; Col. 1:12). You are his "dear one" (he chose you and knows all about you), his "beloved child," and a thousand other wonderful things. When the Holy Spirit speaks to you about yourself, he consistently builds you up, helping you see yourself as he sees you.

Possibly the most striking example of this is in Paul's first letter to the Corinthians. Even though the apostle knew all their sinful and evil ways, led by the Holy Spirit he built them up, right from the start of his letter:

Paul, called as an apostle of Jesus Christ by the will of God, and Sosthenes our brother, to the church of God which is at Corinth, to those who have been sanctified in Christ Jesus, saints by calling, with all who in every place call upon the name of our Lord Jesus Christ, their Lord and ours: Grace to you and peace from God our Father and the Lord Jesus Christ. I thank my God always concerning you, for the grace of God which was given you in Christ Jesus, that in everything you were enriched in Him, in all speech and all knowledge, even as the testimony concerning Christ was confirmed in you, so that you are not lacking in any gift, awaiting eagerly the revelation of our Lord Jesus Christ, who shall also confirm you to the end, blameless in the day of our Lord Jesus Christ. God is faithful, through whom you were called into fellowship with His Son, Jesus Christ our Lord (1 Cor. 1:1–9).

Look at all those positive statements Paul made about the Corinthian believers! It was only after establishing who they are in Jesus Christ that he proceeded to correct their behavior. We find that when Paul wrote to the Corinthians again, they were different: they had begun to discover who they really were in God's eyes.

This is how God deals with us today.

You can recognize God's voice by his explicitness when he is talking about your sins, and you can recognize his voice by the value he places on you when he is talking about your worth as a person.

Knowing God's Voice by What It Tells You About Relating to Others

You can also recognize God's voice when he is talking about others, because he shows you how he sees them.

There was once a man who despised me and told me to my face he would never trust me.

He sat in the front pew every Sunday and glared at me, this deacon who opposed me at every leadership meeting. A large part of the church membership knew what a lemon he was! And I was tempted to get back at him — to get rid of him — to expose him and his duplicity!

But our Lord, in all of his instructions to me, would not let me do anything except try to build a relationship.

The final test came when I was getting ready to go to another pastorate. As I started to drive about 150 miles to a possible place of service, the Lord told me he did not want me to leave this place without seeking to do all I could to make that flawed relationship right.

God instructed me to pray and, on the way home, to look for that deacon, who worked on a power-line crew. Some sixty miles from home, I found him and took him out to lunch, seeking to make everything right. I think I succeeded. Since that time, I have learned to recognize God's voice by what he tells me about others and my relationships with them.

Your relationships with people depend on your perception of them. How can you see others the right way, beneath their masks and the front they present to the world? The answer is to see others with the eyes of Christ.

When God talks to you about others and how you should relate to them, you can be sure he will follow the basic principles he has established. Like those in Philippians 4:8, where God tells us through Paul that he wants us to fill our minds with those things that are good and deserve praise; things that are true, noble, right, pure, lovely, and honorable.

The enemy tries to give us wrong thoughts that result in wrong actions, so that the name of Christ will be discredited by the behavior of Christians to one another. You can recognize some signs that your thinking is from God, not from the Evil One, by the content.

The enemy says, "He doesn't like you." "He's mad at you." "She thinks you're dowdy." "She's too good for you."

God's way sounds like this: "I love her and will pour my love for her through you." Or "He has something good to say. Listen to him." Or "He's hurting. Invite him over for a visit."

God's Way: *Tempering Justice with Mercy and Forgiveness*

There is a phrase of a song that goes like this: "Not my brother, not my sister, but it's me, O Lord, standing in the need of prayer."

You and I don't want judgment from another brother or sister, and they don't want judgment from us. God warns us that judgment will be merciless to one who has shown no mercy.

In all human relationships there is a continuing degree of conflict that is due to our many imperfections. These conflicts become a fertile ground for the enemy to plant seeds in our hearts that will cause division amongst brothers and sisters and bring dishonor to the name of Christ.

If a person has not been to church in three weeks and you say, "Oh, he's turned away from God," that's judging. But perhaps you care enough about him to phone and find out he's depressed because sin has gotten a hold on him. Then, if God tells you to, you go see him, love him, and pray with him, that's mercy.

Or suppose a woman comes to church poorly dressed and you say, "She shouldn't come to church looking like that!" That's judging. But if you talk to her, help her find a job, take her shopping, or make her a dress, that's mercy.

John Sanford reminds us, "God says, 'You do the loving; I'll do the judging.' "

"Brethren, even if a man is caught in any trespass, you who are spiritual, restore such a one in a spirit of gentleness; *each one* looking to yourself, lest you too be tempted. Bear one another's burdens, and thus fulfill the law of Christ" (Gal. 6:1–2).

Conflicts also become an opportunity for the Lord Jesus to build men and women into closer relationships. You can expect the content of our Lord's message to be tempered with mercy and the enemy's to be hardened with revenge.

Jesus had a lot to say about judging. For example: "Do not judge lest you be judged. For in the way you judge, you will be judged; and by your standard of measure, it will be measured to you" (Matt. 7:1–2).

One day Peter asked Jesus about forgiveness: "Lord, how often shall my brother sin against me and I forgive him? Up to seven times?" (Matt. 18:21). He was probably surprised at Jesus' answer: "I do not say to you, up to seven times, but up to seventy times seven" (v. 22).

The Lord's word to you about others will contain these elements:

1. *The good in others.* God will reveal to you the good in others, the things that are of him and by him — the things of good report that are lovely and worthy of praise.
2. *The help you can give to others.* God will reveal to you simple, practical ways whereby you can become a channel of his love toward others.
3. *Forgiveness.* God will show you ways to reach out to the offended
4. *Explanations of why the person acted that way.* When you have stood in another's shoes, it is much easier to extend mercy. God will show you how to help constructively in the other's life.
5. A *consciousness of your own weakness and failures in the past.* This will develop in you a genuine humility towards the other person.

The Evil One's ways are far different from God's ways. Satan's word to you will contain these elements of generalization and retribution:

1. *Value judgments.* A value judgment is a generalized speculation on the basis of an observation (which might not be true). For example, on the basis of one *fact* — "She did not return the dishes she borrowed" — you reach a *value judgment* — "She is a thief and no good."
2. *Revenge.* "What can I do to make them pay for the wrong they have done?"
3. *Degrading thoughts about individuals.*

In summary, what the Lord says to you about others who have wronged you will be full of mercy. You have been commmanded to be as merciful as our heavenly Father is merciful.

TRUTH: A merciful God helps his children to be merciful.

God's Way: Building Relationships, Not Divisions

Our God is vitally concerned with reconciliation — not only of people with himself, but of people with people. Many Scriptures indicate this emphasis on building relationships, and we will look at some of them.

God reminds us of our own alienation from him by emphasizing all that he has done to show his attitude of reconciliation toward us, his children.

"Now all *these* things are from God, who reconciled us to Himself through Christ, and gave us the ministry of reconciliation" (2 Cor. 5:18). Then, lest we still don't understand, Paul goes on: "Namely, that God was in Christ reconciling the world to Himself, not counting their trespasses against them, and He has committed to us the word of reconciliation" (v. 19).

Jesus tells us that our problems with others affect our relationship with him. He says, "If therefore you are presenting your offering at the altar, and there remember that your brother has something against you, leave your offering there before the altar, and go your way; first be reconciled to your brother, and then come and present your offering" (Matt. 5:23–24).

As God speaks to you about a brother or a sister, you can know his voice by the fact that he will give you thoughts that will work to bring you together. Our love for one another is evidence that we have heard him. "All people will know that you are my followers," he says, "if you love each other."

From your heavenly Father, you can expect to hear:

1. Reasons why you need to get together
2. Ways in which you can build bridges to others
3. Ways in which you can worship with them
4. The worth of our brothers and sisters to him and to us

Satan's attempt at causing division in the body of Christ has centered on three areas. You can expect him to use them with you and thereby betray you. Be aware of the following threats to fellowship and the unity of believers.

1. *The enemy uses doctrine to divide.* There are seven thousand denominations in the world today, and each member would say that his or her group has a doctrinal basis. Certain fundamental beliefs unite some groups, but they divide more or less sharply on others. Although doctrine (truth) is important, there are a few things to remember.

1. None of us has all the truth about any one doctrine.
2. Perceptions of truth are progressively revised as one becomes more and more mature (see John 16:12–14).
3. Perceptions of truth are tempered by one's spiritual gifts. The prophet does not see things in the same way as the pastor, yet both are important to the body of Christ.

The enemy will seek to use *your* understanding of truth to separate you from those who do not have the same perception. It has always humbled me to remember that our Lord has seen fit to use people who have opposing views of truth to mine.

2. *The enemy uses experience to divide.* Spiritual experiences are wonderful and seem to vary from Christian to Christian. The Lord does not allow everyone to participate in the same way. While valid to an individual, these spiritual experiences are not a basis for fellowship, although the enemy seeks to use them as such.

A supernatural experience from God is determined by such things as personality type or level of maturity in Christ. It can also be God's sovereign decision to give a spiritual experience for a purpose of his own determination. These extraordinary experiences are valid, but our fellowship with him is not dependent on them. Nor are they a measure of our own "spirituality."

Only three of the disciples saw Moses and Elijah with Jesus on the Mount of Transfiguration. Where were the other nine? Elsewhere, experiencing whatever God had for them!

The enemy seeks to divide Christians by making us perceive spiritual experiences as a measure of maturity or of closeness to God or of God's blessings on an individual. Because of the influence of the enemy, God's children — you and I and all the others — have these tendencies:

1. We look down on those who have not had a particular experience.
2. We demand that others have the same experience. This is a sure way to divide those who do and those who don't! It also promotes hypocrisy in those who pretend to have had the experience in order to be accepted.
3. We divide ourselves into groups, identifying with those who have had similar experiences to our own.

3. *The enemy uses different methods to divide.* The enemy also seeks to divide people by the way they do ministry and Christian service. It is easy to become convinced that our way of ministering is the only right way and that everybody else is wrong.

But is there only one right way? Yes, when it comes to salvation. The Bible states that Jesus is the only one who can save us. His name is the only power in the world that has been given for our salvation. And we must be saved through him.

However, our Lord used many options. He healed the blind by one touch. By two touches. And by the dirt-and-spittle method. He is the same today — not boxed in by your ideas or mine of how he should work. Or what he should do. Or where. Or when.

"Now there are varieties of gifts, but the same Spirit. And there are varieties of ministries, and the same Lord. And there are varieties of effects, but the same God who works all things in all *persons.* But to each one is given the manifestation of the Spirit for the common good" (1 Cor. 12:4–7).

Knowing God's Voice by What the Content Tells us About Faith

"Faith" means trusting God, not what our senses tell us. One of the ways we know his voice is that its content is such that he keeps us at a point of trusting him for something new — in ourselves, in our loved ones, in our ministry. Trusting him for deeper levels. For more growth. For wider usage. And always advancing from faith to faith.

Since faith is of such vital importance to the whole Christian experience, you may really expect to hear a lot from God on this matter, for faith comes from hearing the words of God.

From what you have already read, you know that God is still working with me and teaching me. Possibly you have also sensed that one of the fruits he is trying to grow in my life is patience. Taking that into consideration, I would like to ask you, "Are you like I am? Wanting to have *everything* where I can have it through my senses: see it, touch it, hear it *now?*"

From personal experience, I can testify that God is continually working with us on the matter of patience. He loves faith and wants us in a faith posture all the time. When our faith becomes a reality and he has us trusting him in all matters, we move on from one level of faith to another.

Johnnie and I have five children, now aged 35, 34, 33, 24, and 16. With all of them, God has called us to trust him — trust him at the different ages, with different situations, and for different levels of life.

There is Susan. She has many of the same characteristics as her father (which God has been working on). She is given to extremes in some things to the detriment of others.

God has kept us at points of trust for Susan all her life. We had to trust him for her salvation while she was in junior high. There were other times we entrusted God with her welfare:

In senior high, for her protection from evil

In college, for guidance for a life's goal

In her first job, for right friends

In her social life, for the right husband

In business (where she is now), for a right balance

At every level God was faithful to fulfill what we had asked him for, and he continues to be faithful. But he keeps us in a position of faith through it all.

Dr. Charles Stanley writes: "God is always challenging our faith and in so doing He builds our relationship with Him and helps us grow into intimacy with Him. When Jesus was on earth, He was always looking for people to respond in faith. He could just speak and that would be the end of it, but in many instances His voice requires an act of faith on our part to comprehend what He has revealed."[2]

God speaks to us in a million ways, but one of the clearest is through his Word. However, his messages to you in Scripture reach you only if you open the Holy Book. When you do, two things may happen:

He may give you his "Logos" (general word). *Logos* is Greek for the general word of God. The whole Bible is God's Logos. It tells about God's plans, his purposes, and his principles. The more you absorb of his Logos, the better you will know him.

He may give you a "Rhema" (specific word). *Rhema,* on the other hand, is Greek for a specific word from God. You may be reading along in the Bible or may suddenly remember a verse. In either case a passage becomes so meaningful that you sense God's speaking to you. A *rhema* is a promise that God has definite plans for a situation or problem.

For example, a woman in my congregation had a rebellious son. One morning she was reading along in Isaiah when she came to a word God had specially meant for her:

I have seen his [willful] ways, but I will heal him; I will lead him and restore comfort to him and to his mourners (Isa. 57:18).

How that *rhema* comforted this mother through the next years, as her son continued to rebel! Sometimes she became frightened for him, but then she would remember the verse and thank God for his plan. Finally the young man repented and is now himself receiving *rhemas* from God.

God Bolsters Our Faith

When God speaks about faith, you can be sure it is God speaking, because of certain characteristics of what he says:

1. The word is in line with scriptural principles.
2. The word will cause you to trust him more.

2. Charles Stanley, *How to Listen to God* (Nashville, Tenn.: Oliver-Nelson Books, 1985), p. 53.

3. The word could be repeated and expanded as you go back to the Lord about it.

Since Abraham is used in the Bible as the prime example of faith, it will be good for us to examine this patriarch's faith experience. We will see the Lord making a promise, repeating it, and enlarging on it.

First, God gave Abram a command: "Go forth from your country, and from your relatives and from your father's house, to the land which I will show you (Gen. 12:1).

Then God promised Abram, "I will make you a great nation, and I will bless you, and make your name great; and so you shall be a blessing; and I will bless those who bless you, and the one who curses you I will curse. And in you all the families of the earth shall be blessed" (Gen. 12:2–3).

Later on, when Abram and his nephew, Lot, finally parted company, God expanded the promise to include territory. "Now lift up your eyes and look from the place where you are, northward and southward and eastward and westward; for all the land which you see, I will give it to you and to your descendants forever" (Gen. 13:14–15). Then he also enlarged on what he had meant about Abram's descendants, saying, "I will make your descendants as the dust of the earth; so that if anyone can number the dust of the earth, then your descendants can also be numbered" (v. 16).

There were both good times and hard times for Abram in his new land, culminating in the daring surprise rescue of Lot and all that the enemy had stolen. After that happened, God repeated his promise about the land. "I am the LORD who brought you out of Ur of the Chaldeans to give you this land to possess it" (Gen. 15:7).

Then came the traumatic events surrounding Abram's attempts to "help God" keep his promise of many descendants (Gen. 16).

Thirteen years after the slave girl Hagar bore Abram a son (Ishmael), God reiterated and expanded his promise. "I will make you exceedingly fruitful, and I will make nations of you, and kings shall come forth from you. And I will establish My covenant between Me and you and your descendants after you throughout their generations for an everlasting covenant, to be God to you and to your descendants after you. And I will give to you and to your descendants after you, the land of your sojournings, all the land of Canaan, for an everlasting possession; and I will be their God" (Gen. 17:6–8).

As the Lord reinforced and blessed Abraham, so he will reinforce and bless you.

The Enemy Attacks Our Faith

God is very much aware of the enemy's attack on your faith. Satan will attack and bombard your faith by pointing your thoughts in certain directions to get you to doubt both God's goodness and what God has said.

Enemy Bombardment #1: Pointing you to the negatives of your own and others' past experiences. The enemy distorts your thinking into saying such things as:

"I remember what happened the last time I did this!"

"I remember what happened when [name] did this!"

Enemy Bombardment #2: Pointing you to the "limitations" of your present circumstances. The enemy also perverts your thoughts about what is happening now:

"That can never happen: there are too many obstacles in the way."

"I can't do it. Let someone else try."

"I've tried, and it doesn't make any difference. I give up!"

As a child of God, know that your faith *will* be attacked by the Evil One. But know also that our Lord stands by his word and that he will keep you focused on himself and his promises if you ask and trust that he will answer. Victorious in faith? Or defeated by the enemy? The choice is yours!

I hope you will choose to say with Paul:

> We do not lose heart, but though our outer man is decaying, yet our inner man is being renewed day by day. For momentary, light affliction is producing for us an eternal weight of glory far beyond all comparison, while we look not at the things which are seen, but at the things which are not seen; for the things which are seen are temporal, but the things which are not seen are eternal (2 Cor. 4:16–18).

I invite you to join me in "fixing our eyes on Jesus, the author and perfecter of faith" (Heb. 12:2).

Jesus is
　rivers of living water.

He is like
　streams which flow through dry places
　to irrigate the land and enable it to be fruitful.

He does this
　in us
　in His Holy Spirit

Jesus says . . .
　out of the desert of your life
　shall burst forth the abundance of My life,
　rivers of living water,

　if you
　seek Me
　　with all your heart, soul, mind, and strength.

These rivers cannot be contained,
　but must flow to the ocean of humanity,
　feeding people around you
　with all the good things I have given you . . .[1]

1. Sarah Hornsby, *At the Name of Jesus* (Grand Rapids: Chosen Books [Zondervan], 1983), September 12.

11

Knowing God's Voice
by the Results It Produces

How else can I know God's voice — that those words and thoughts come from him? How can I be sure it is God who causes me to think in a certain way?

One of the surest ways to recognize God's voice is the effect the words produce in you. The results of hearing God's voice center around increased faith and *gratitude*.

God's Voice Will Bring You Encouragement

One evening as I was walking up the path of a home in which there was a young Christian mother struggling with an alcohol problem, I sought the guidance of the Lord to get her to listen to me. And he told me what to do. . . .

After I had entered the home and gotten through the formalities, she said to me, "Here I am, a Christian with all these problems. Yet my husband is not a Christian and lives much better than I do. What can I do?"

"The Lord Jesus has instructed me," I replied, "to get you to talk to him and ask him a few questions." After a few simple instructions about the Holy Spirit and his presence in her, I instructed the woman to ask the Lord about his thoughts of her.

After a few moments of silence she told me, "He said 'You are much more valuable than you think you are.'"

Instructing her again, I said, "Ask him how valuable you are."

When she did, she came up with this amazing answer: "He said that I am as valuable as he is."

I could see she was perplexed by what God had told her, so I explained to her that the "value" of anything is determined by the price a person is willing to pay for it. I reminded her that Scripture says Christ has given his life for us (e.g., Gal. 1:4) — which means that he sees us as valuable as himself.

Light began to dawn. She was amazed at what God had told her, and there was new hope shining in her eyes.

Her husband was flabbergasted upon hearing this great truth and could see that there had been no manipulation. In the next ten minutes he received Christ as his Lord and Savior!

The point I want to make here is that we know his voice by the fact that he encourages us in every way he can. Our Lord did not approve of this woman's self-inflicted problem, but he approved of *her* — and he was encouraging her, for he saw she needed acceptance and verification of her worth.

Ninety percent of what God says to me is encouragement. I do not know if this percentage is due to the fact that discouragement has been the major tactic of the devil in my life. Or just that the Lord, who walked in our shoes, knows our constant need of encouragement. Maybe both.

What I do know is that I have never come away from hearing God without being encouraged. I have learned that discouragement does not come from him. Paul wrote to the Corinthian church, "Blessed *be* the God and Father of our Lord Jesus Christ, the Father of mercies and God of all comfort; who comforts us in all our affliction . . ." (2 Cor. 1:3–4).

In how many ways and forms does his encouragement come to me! It may be through a Scripture recalled from my memory bank, a Scripture interpretation for a present circumstances, or a "new" Scripture I had never noticed before.

Sometimes I am encouraged through reminders of his promises to me. Or a word for the moment. A look from his point of view.

As we have wrestled through problems with one of our children and this child's lack of interest in God and his ways, we have been burdened by bad behavior patterns. The Lord encouraged me through it all by reminding me of the promise he had given me: that this child would be used in his redemptive purpose.

Whatever the method, the Lord encourages me to keep on keeping on. He assures me it will all turn out well, according to his plan. He spurs me on to take the next step, so that without hesitation I can join Paul in saying, "He is the God of all encouragement!"

On the other hand, the enemy attacks us with discouragement. This is one of Satan's main weapons. He constantly seeks to discourage you and thereby make you impotent: to cause you to stop what you are doing or to do things in a halfhearted way.

The enemy will point to and distort present appearances and past experiences. He will remind you of the time that has lapsed since you last received a word from the Lord. And he will punctuate his attack with a full-color show of your past failures.

Be aware of Satan's tactics. And remember that a sure sign that you have heard God's voice is that you are comforted and uplifted — encouraged to love him, to trust him, and to follow him.

God's Voice Will Bring You Peace

What God says will never cause you to worry or fret. The God who tells you, "Do not worry," is the God who calms your mind and soul. A sure sign you have heard from him is the peace you feel even in the midst of the storm.

Our eldest son had a drug problem. He was away from home, living with a group of people on drugs, and getting into more and more trouble. He was finally arrested. The desk sergeant at the jail called us at 5:00 A.M. with the news.

All through the crisis we had a peaceful assurance — because God had spoken and was continuing to speak — that Richard would come back. Peace in the storm by his presence and his voice!

One of the results of hearing God, and receiving what he has said, is peace. If a person's thinking is controlled by the Spirit, then there is life and peace. You can know beyond any shadow of doubt that when you worry or are afraid, it is because you have not heard God.

God commands us not to worry and then he gives the positive solution to worry: "Be anxious for nothing, but in everything by prayer and supplication with thanksgiving let your requests be made known to God. And the peace of God, which surpasses all comprehension, shall guard your hearts and your minds in Christ Jesus" (Phil. 4:6–7).

This "peace" is an inner tranquility in a situation clamoring for attention. A light in the impenetrable darkness. A calm assurance in impossible circumstances. An unexplainable rest in the midst of chaos.

Jesus had just told his disciples that they would cry and be sad and the world would be happy; that their sadness would become joy, but they would be scattered. Seeing the dismay and perplexity in their faces, he asured them that they — and we — can have peace in Him despite our circumstances.

"In the world you have tribulation, take courage; I have overcome the world!" (John 16:33b).

Peace. The songwriter's testimony is "No storm can swallow the ship where lies the master of ocean and earth and skies."[2]

You can have peace because of the Lord's presence, his promises, and his power. Because ". . . He Himself has said, 'I will never desert you, nor will I ever forsake you,' so that we confidently say, 'The Lord is my helper, I will not be afraid. What shall man do to me?' " (Heb. 13:5–6).

Jesus, who often commanded his disciples, "Fear not," will not in any way cause you fear or worry.

This peace from God our Father and the Lord Jesus Christ is often inexplicable to others and even to yourself. It is a sign you have heard from him, so listen to God until you have reached a point of peace. Remember, too, that any and every thought of worry and fear comes not from the Lord but from the enemy.

God's Voice Will Bring You Sympathetic Understanding

There is a woman in our church who writes more letters to me than anyone else. Most of the letters are nasty in a "religious" way. Sometimes they are selfish or caustic, even threatening. My natural inclination would be to avoid that person when I see her.

But, as I spoke to the Lord about this, he said, "What she has written is often not from me — that is her "flesh" expressing itself. She likes to do it in letter writing. But you, Peter Lord, have flesh expressions in a different way," God added. "How do you want

2. "Master, the Tempest Is Raging," Mary A. Baker.

people to act toward you after you have administered a 'flesh kick'? Treat her in the same way."

Well, I want people to be kind, forgiving, and loving to me after I have indulged in a "flesh kick," so that's how I am dealing with this person.

This is what God's voice has told me to do. He will tell you something similar.

You will know God is speaking to you about others because of your new attitude of understanding toward them and the actions you want to take. You will begin to want to love them. Then, as he continues to speak and you listen, the Lord will supply the love.

You will feel compassion for other people. Want to be with them. Want to extend mercy to them, forgive them, and be a blessing to them. You will find yourself interceding for them and expressing love to them through words of encouragement and helping actions. When God speaks to you about others, he will cause you to see them as he sees them, to love them as he loves them.

But the enemy again moves in against us, with attacks on your mind that are aimed at contradicting what God has told you:

1. *The enemy puts thoughts in your mind that cause you to judge someone.* Remember the admonition: "Who are you to judge the servant of another? To his own master he stands or falls; and stand he will, for the Lord is able to make him stand" (Rom. 14:4).

2. *The enemy puts thoughts in your mind that cause you to despise someone.* Paul, in writing to the Roman believers, questions us, too: "But you, why do you judge your brother? Or you again, why do you regard your brother with contempt? For we shall all stand before the judgment seat of God" (Rom. 14:10).

3. *The enemy puts thoughts in your mind that cause you to reject someone.* There is a measuring stick about rejecting someone that we rarely use: Christ accepted you with lovingkindness; so you should accept others in the same spirit. This will bring glory to God.

4. *The enemy puts thoughts in your mind that cause you to speak evil of someone.* James, who had much to say about the Christian use of the tongue, warned us about this, too, in his letter to believers:

Do not speak against one another, brethren. He who speaks against a brother, or judges his brother, speaks against the law, and judges the law; but if you judge the law, you are not a doer of the law, but a judge *of it* (James 4:11).

5. *The enemy puts thoughts in your mind that cause you to carry a grudge against someone.* James also said, "Do not complain, brethren, against one another, that you yourselves may not be judged; behold, the judge is standing right at the door" (James 5:9).

When you are listening to God, you will hear him say, "Try to do what makes peace and helps one another." If you receive those words, you will not judge others nor hold them in contempt nor despise them nor reject them nor criticize them nor curse them. These things are not from the Lord.

You may surprise yourself because you will have compassion for others. You will receive them and be merciful to them. You will forgive, seek to save them, bless them, and intercede for them.

You will find yourself praying things like: "Father, but for your grace, I would be there." Or "Lord, show me how I can help." Or "What do you want me to do for them, Jesus?" Love, mercy, and compassion will rise in you, as will a desire to draw closer to others in order to help them.

You can be absolutely sure that God, who has clearly commanded you not to judge another, will never tell you things about other people for the sake of judgment. If he tells you anything about others, it will be so that you can intercede in their behalf and reach out to help them.

God's Voice Will Bring You Hope

When God speaks, do you hear a loving father who forgives you and has a real interest in you? Or do you hear a demanding parent who is always expecting you to measure up to higher and higher expectations?

When you pray, do you come as to a loving, accepting father? Or do you feel condemned and never able to live up to God's expectations?

The God of the Bible is *love*, which brings hope. And when he speaks, the results will flow out of his love for you.

The years of 1972 to 1976 were the very hardest I had ever experienced in the ministry. I know now that God was doing a work of purifying and pruning in my life during that time.

The attacks of the enemy allowed by God — Norman Grubb calls him "God's devil" — were centered in hopelessness. Satan sought to drive me with a sense of hopelessness about my life and my ministry. I was often filled with despair.

What kept me afloat, what kept me going, were the times I shared alone with God. Times when he gave me hope and a reason to live.

The situation did not really change much. But in those times, when I let him, God always lifted me up

. . . with hope that he was there

. . . with hope that he was doing the best he could for me

. . . with hope that he was giving me what I had asked him for: a Christian character.

Of course, I wanted it all in a painless, costless, quick way — but that is not God's way. And I have been able to see something of the reasons why he doesn't work that way.

"Hope." What does this word mean in God's vocabulary? If we can conclude what God means when he uses that word in the Bible, it will help us identify his voice.

Unger's *Bible Dictionary* defines "hope" as "the expectation of good." Vines says, "It is a favorable and sure expectation It has to do with the unseen of the future. The happy anticipation of good."

The opposite of hope is "hopelessness," which Webster says refers to "having no expectation of good or success; despairing; despondent."

How do you know where *hope* about the future comes from? Is it from God? As in the other results of listening to God's voice, here, too, God has given signs to direct you:

1. *Joy and peace accompany hope from God.* This interactive circle is emphasized by Paul's prayer to the Roman believers: "Now may the God of hope fill you with all joy and peace in believing, that you may abound in hope by the power of the Holy Spirit" (Rom. 15:13).

2. *When hope is from God, there is rejoicing.* "Rejoice always; pray without ceasing; in everything give thanks; for this is God's will for you in Christ Jesus. . . . Faithful is He who calls you, and He also will bring it to pass" (1 Thess. 5:16–18, 24).

3. *Hope brings boldness of speech.* Referring to the much greater glory of Christ's new way, which will continue forever, Paul says, "Having therefore such a hope, we use great boldness in *our* speech" (2 Cor. 3:12).

4. *Steadfastness is also a part of this hope.* Imagine praying for some-

one and saying, "We always thank God for the things you have done because of your faith. And we thank him for the work you have done because of your love. And we thank him that you continue to be steadfast and strong because of your hope in our Lord Jesus Christ" (1 Thess. 1:3).

5. *There is no disappointment in this hope from God.* We have been made right with God because of our faith, and we have peace with God through our Lord Jesus Christ. Through our faith, Christ has brought us into that blessing of God's grace that we now enjoy. Our happy hope of sharing God's glory "does not disappoint, because the love of God has poured out within our hearts through the Holy Spirit who was given to us" (Rom. 5:5).

By way of contrast, consider the enemy's tactic of putting thoughts in your mind that cause you to feel hopeless and discouraged. Hopelessness manifests itself with such thoughts as: "It will never work out." "Nothing good is ever going to happen." "It's no use." "I'll never change." "It won't do any good." "Nothing will make a difference."

Based on God's Word, you can say to the enemy, "It is *God* who makes the difference!" God will fill you when you allow him to, so that you may abound in hope by the Holy Spirit.

Hope coming from the Father is the assurance that what we are trusting him for — on the basis of his character and word — will come to pass. The object of the hope brought by the Father is such a sure thing that we can rejoice in it before it actually comes, for its coming is as certain as the dawn. His promise is always "I will not fail you."

This hope is not wishful thinking. Neither is it daydreaming nor optimism. This hope comes to you as you listen to God's voice, because the Father will reveal himself to you. This hope comes to you as he reveals his intention for you and renews his promises.

God's Voice Will Create and Sustain Your Faith

In 1952 the Lord Jesus spoke plainly to my wife and me. He said, "Go to seminary. Go to New Orleans. Go at the end of the school year to summer school."

The deacons in our church in Belleview, Florida, sought to discourage us. The church was experiencing revival. God's blessings were being poured out. They reminded me that I had no visible means of support, no savings, and they emphasized the fact of my responsibility to our two small children.

They were right in everything they said.

But the Lord had spoken, so I went, leaving the family behind, for I had no job and no place to live. There was a quiet inner confidence, a peace I could not explain.

My first day in New Orleans the following things happened:

I landed a job.

I registered for summer school.

I found a place to live.

I called home to tell my wife about all this, and she told me that a church from Mississippi had called to say they wanted me as pastor.

The glory of God descended in that phone booth!

The point I want to make here is that when God speaks, you have faith. It's a faith you cannot explain to others or to yourself. It's just there. As long as you reflect on his words, the faith remains.

The Scriptures picture faith as all-important to our God and Lord:

1. He is the God who *demands* faith: "The righteous man *shall* live by faith" (Rom. 1:17).
2. He is the God who *desires* faith: "Where is your faith?" (Luke 8:25).
3. He is the God who *delights* in faith: "Without faith it is impossible to please Him" (Heb. 11:6).
4. He is also the God who *gives the basis and reason for faith* when he speaks with us: "So faith *comes* from hearing, and hearing by the word of Christ" (Rom. 10:17).

One sign that you have heard from God is that faith rises in your heart. *You believe!* You believe in spite of what you sense or perceive and in spite of what your reasoning tells you. You believe easily and naturally, for you have heard the One whom you know as God.

Faith is both *created* by the Lord's word to us and *sustained* by that word. He initiates our faith and is also the completer, the finisher of our faith (Heb. 12:2).

Enemy Tactic: Thoughts of Doubt, Unbelief, Suspicion, Anxiety, and Skepticism. Satan wants you to listen to him and depend only on your feelings or figurings. These distortions — if allowed to prevail — will lead to disobedience:

1. the disobedience of inactivity caused by doubt
2. the disobedience of wrong activity
3. the disobedience of complacency

However, when the Father speaks and you listen and accept what he says, you will find faith rising up in your heart. You will have these assurances:

1. hopeful assurance that what is now invisible will become visible when God is ready to show it to you
2. joyful assurance that makes you sing at midnight
3. obedient assurance that causes you to cooperate in whatever way he asks

One of the sure results of hearing God is faith: resting faith, steadfast faith, rejoicing faith.

God's Voice Will Produce Gratitude in Your Heart

One morning I was meditating on Psalm 138:8: "The LORD will accomplish what concerns me; Thy lovingkindness, O LORD, is everlasting; do not forsake the works of Thy hands."

> The Lord spoke to me and said: My child, I have invested too much in you to forsake you. You are the object of my creative and redemptive plan. It is fellowship with *me* that I designed you for, created you for, reclaimed you for.
>
> When I sent my Son into this world, it was to demonstrate to you the possibility of fellowship with me where you are. It was also to make fellowship possible by taking care of sin that prevented it.
>
> As you read the Scriptures, do you not see that my Son Jesus and

I always had fellowship together? That is why when he bore your sins, and I had to forsake him, he suffered such agony.

Would it have been agony if he had not been used to having fellowship with me? No! In eternity he had fellowship with me. In a human body on earth, among people and conditions like you live in, he had fellowship with me. And so can you.

No, I will not forsake you. More than that, I will finish the perfection for which I called you — both as an individual and as part of my bride, the church.

Your need is not to be concerned about my forsaking you, but about your being preoccupied and forsaking me.

My heart overflowed with thanksgiving and praise to God for those words to me. And always when I listen to him, I am grateful and full of thanksgiving to him for himself and his words.

Thanksgiving and praise flow from grateful hearts. A grateful heart cannot help overflowing with thanks and offering praise.

Old Testament Praise

The Old Testament is full of praises to God. Look at the exultation in Deuteronomy:

To the LORD your God belong heaven and the highest heavens, the earth and all that is in it.... For the LORD your God is the God of gods and the Lord of lords, the great, the mighty, and the awesome God who does not show partiality, nor take a bribe.... He is your praise and He is your God, who has done these great and awesome things for you which your eyes have seen (Deut. 10:14, 17, 21).

And we can join in David's triumphant song:

Blessed art Thou, O LORD God of Israel our father, forever and ever. Thine, O LORD, is the greatness and the power and the glory and the victory and the majesty, indeed everything that is in the heavens and the earth; Thine is the dominion, O LORD, and Thou dost exalt Thyself as head over all. Both riches and honor *come* from Thee, and Thou dost rule over all, and in Thy hand is power and might; and it lies in Thy hand to make great, and to strengthen everyone. Now therefore, our God, we thank Thee, and praise Thy glorious name (1 Chron. 29:10–13).

When you have allowed Him to speak to you — to guide, explain, comfort, and love you — gratitude will arise in your heart. And this gratitude makes expression easy, desirable, and beautiful. You will praise him as did the psalmist:

> I will give Thee thanks with all my heart; I will sing praises to thee before the gods. I will bow down toward Thy holy temple, and give thanks to Thy name for Thy lovingkindness and Thy truth; for Thou hast magnified Thy word according to all Thy name (Ps. 138:1–2).

New Testament Praise

In the New Testament, the Scriptures command, "Pray without ceasing; in everything give thanks; for this is God's will for you in Christ Jesus" (1 Thess. 5:17–18; cf. Phil. 4:6).

Impossible, you think? It depends on your concept of prayer! It *is* impossible to "never stop praying" if you think that to pray means to talk to God — with *you* doing the talking. However, what this Scripture commands is fully possible if you understand prayer as basically listening.

If you listen (pray) without stopping, you will be able to give thanks in everything. God's words to you — while not always explanations — are always such that you can give thanks to him that he is present. That he is in charge. That he loves you and is concerned about your welfare. That he is always working things together for your best.

Enemy Tactic: Thoughts of Ingratitude, Envy, Jealousy, and Covetousness. The enemy will remind you of what you do not have. He will whisper that what others have you should have, too. He sneers, "After all, you deserve it!" And he will put in your mind all the other negative thoughts that reflect ingratitude.

Paul, writing to Timothy, warns that ingratitude — unthankfulness — will be one of the signs of the perilous times of "the last days" (2 Tim. 3:1–2).

How good to know that the Holy Spirit will bring to mind those things that will put gratitude in your heart and a song on your lips. For he will point to the Lord Jesus Christ as the source of all good things.

A mouth that praises and thanks our heavenly Father is evidence of a grateful heart, a heart filled with thanksgiving that we are hearing the One who has pronounced through Paul that "... God causes all things to work together for good to those who love God ..." (Rom. 8:28).

"Through Him then, let us continually offer up a sacrifice of praise to God, that is, the fruit of lips that give thanks to his name" (Heb. 13:15).

4

Receiving God's Signals

... whatever is true,
whatever is right,
whatever is lovely,
whatever is noble,
whatever is pure,
whatever is admirable,
— if anything is excellent or praiseworthy —
think about such things.

St. Paul
Philippians 4:8, NIV

12

Processes of the Thought World

Y ou would never believe what I have been thinking!"
"I just had a wild idea!"
"I just had a thought out of the blue. . . ."

Have you ever made one of these statements or a similar one?
Have you heard somebody else say anything like this? Of course
you have!

All of these statements indicate that we are sometimes surprised
at our own thoughts.

Think about this. Your thoughts are proceeding along an orderly
path; then suddenly comes a thought that is not a part of that
pattern of thinking. And you may say, "I just thought of something!"
or words to that effect. Our speech is filled with phrases indicating
that we all have random thoughts for no apparent reason.

What bearing does our thought life have on the physical world
and the spiritual world? How does the spiritual world interact with
the physical world? How does God — or the devil — work his will on
earth? What is the usual, ordinary way that this happens?

More specifically, how does God minister love to a person,
whether directly or indirectly? Does he not do it through the mind
of man? If God wants to minister his love to me directly, he usually
does it by placing thoughts in my mind as I allow him. If I receive
those thoughts and act on them, I experience his love.

"It is a well-known axiom of the psychology of perception," says

Benedict J. Groeschel, "that we succeed in listening only if we respond in some way to what we hear."[1]

If God wants to minister to me through someone else, he usually places a thought in that person's mind about something to say or to do. When he or she receives it and obeys, I am ministered to by God through another.

How does the devil get his will done? How does he slander a person? Murder someone? I have never known of a person slandered or murdered directly by Satan. But there are many people harmed by other people after the devil has put evil ideas in their minds.

The first step of the spiritual world's interaction with the physical world is most often a thought placed in the mind of an individual. It is not usually by audible sounds that God speaks to us these days. The Lord communicates in our thought life and through the Holy Spirit's interpreting the Scriptures to us, as we have seen in the introduction to this book.

How important, then, it is for us to understand certain basic things about our thought life. This is natural and scriptural, for God lives inside our minds and hearts — in our thought world.

The Importance of Our Thought Life

My attitude at any given moment is determined by my thoughts. If I am afraid, loving, anxious, peaceful or filled by any other such feeling, it is all dependent on my thoughts. So also is it with everyone.

1. *Our thoughts produce our attitudes.* It is possible to be fearful when there is nothing to be afraid of, simply because you are thinking wrong thoughts. On the other hand, it is possible to be at peace when there is something you *should* be afraid of, but you are not aware of the danger.

2. *Our thoughts precede our attitudes*, whether or not there is any reality to those thoughts. Before we do anything, we think. Before we act, we think. It might be just a split-second reaction, or there

1. Benedict J. Groeschel, O.F.M., Cap., *Listening at Prayer* (New York: Paulist Press, 1984), p. 3.

may be a long time between thoughts and actions. But there is always a thought process prior to an action.

The enemy's attack consists basically in placing untrue thoughts in our mind and calling them "truth," so that we will live according to his purpose and desire. The only power the Evil One has over us is through our thoughts.

Satan told Eve she would find life in eating the forbidden fruit. She believed him and ate and found death instead (Gen. 3). He did not force her hand to pick the fruit nor pry open her mouth to eat it. He just put the idea in her head.

The "big lie" that he uses to hold most Americans captive is that life consists of the abundance of the material things that a man has (cf. Luke 12:15). Believing this, many people act on the assumption that possessions will make them happy. Sometimes they do not discover the truth in a whole lifetime and so live all their days by Satan's lie.

We will inevitably become what we think about all day. This is a commonly accepted psychological truth, and the writer of Hebrews states its logical conclusion unequivocably: "Fixing our eyes on Jesus, the author and perfecter of faith . . ." (Heb. 12:2a).

And Paul adds, "But we all, with unveiled face beholding as in a mirror the glory of the Lord, are being transformed into the same image from glory to glory, just as from the Lord, the Spirit" (2 Cor. 3:18).

The key is that as we are looking at Jesus, the Lord, he is working a step-by-step transformation in us. If we want to be like him, it is imperative that we understand our thought life and learn to control it.

Controlling Our Thought Life

Is it possible to get all the air out of a glass?

Yes, it's easy. Just fill the glass with water.

Is it possible to control our thought life, to control what we think? Can we ever bring "every thought captive" to Christ? (2 Cor. 10:5).

Yes, that's easy, too, if we fill our minds with different thoughts. The principle is the same as filling a glass with water to "control" — get rid of — the air.

Let us consider three simple facts about thinking:

1. We cannot chose *not* to think.
2. We cannot think two thoughts at the same time.
3. We *can* chose our thoughts.

All thoughts can be divided into two basic categories: true and false. The thoughts that come from God are true. He is the God of all truth and has sent the Holy Spirit to dwell in us and to guide us into all truth.

If I can receive God's thoughts, I can think the truth. Therefore I will have the right attitudes and actions.

How do you get the air out of a glass? By filling it with water. How do you get rid of wrong and untrue thoughts? By filling your mind with true and right thoughts from God. The control of our thought life, then, comes by thinking God's thoughts with him.

The Capacities of the Mind

There are three basic mental capacities relevant to fellowship with God that all normal people possess: the capacity to remember, the capacity to receive new information, and the capacity to reason.

Because of their importance in understanding our thought life, we will consider each capacity individually.

The Capacity to Remember

Picture a family reunion, the first in a long time. Laughter, exclamations, people milling around and going from one small group to another. Everyone seems to be talking at once.

"Remember the time. . . ."

"Whatever happened to . . .?"

"So the old schoolhouse finally got torn down!"

"Al looks better than ever, doesn't he? He used to be so. . . ."

The members of that family are using an ability of the mind that God has given us: the capacity to remember.

Earlier I compared the conscious mind to a glass filled with thoughts. Continuing this simile, the subconscious mind can be compared to a deep reservoir into which are emptied and stored all the streams of past experiences and all the brooks of "knowledge" (true *and* false) that have been fed into it.

Those folks at the family reunion were each lowering the glass bucket of the conscious mind into the reservoir of the subconscious. Then they brought up a composite of the thoughts and experiences about their family life and history that had been stored there.

We all do it. When there is a need to think so we can act, we let the bucket down into the well of our thoughts and bring up anything that is related to the matter in hand. Whatever is down in the well (the subconscious) will come up in the bucket (the conscious), including truth, falsehood, and that most dangerous type of lie: untruth that has a mixture of truth in it.

Therefore, the person who decides to act on the basis of the past (what is in the reservoir) is a prisoner of his or her previous experiences and/or knowledge. If the streams and brooks have been pure and true, this is good. If they have been contaminated and wrong, it is bad. Faced with a need for some kind of action, it is vital that we determine what in our bucket is true and what is untrue.

The Christian who wishes to please God must live beyond the knowledge and experience of his reservoir of the subconscious. The examination of our thought world — what the Bible calls "bringing every thought captive to Christ" — is of utmost importance to the believer. But, before going further into that, we must consider another capacity of the mind, since the ability to remember is never static but is always influenced by new and changing input.

The Capacity to Receive New Information

Comparing the mind now to a computer, we can say it has the capacity to receive new information. There are new thoughts and knowledge that cover areas we have never been in before, areas for which there is nothing stored in our memory bank.

Some new ideas and information enlarge and expand areas where we already have some experience. Others contradict the old thoughts stored in our computer-mind.

When we recognize and accept the appropriate thoughts as truth from God, we repent. We change our minds. We reprogram our computer. We haul out the garbage of our wrong thinking and enter the new information that comes from God in its place.

Remember that any new thoughts coming into our conscious minds will find their way down into our subconscious. There they will be catalogued, regardless of whether they are truth or error, and they will affect our future behavior.

The more the subconscious is filled with truth, the easier it will be to live the Christian life and please our God. "Do not be conformed to this world, but be transformed by the renewal of your mind, that you may prove what the will of God is, that which is good and acceptable and perfect" (Rom. 12:2).

There are many channels by which we receive new thoughts and information. Books. Counselors and friends. Television, radio, and even billboards. Our observation of nature, life events, and people.

But, while there are many channels of knowledge, there are only two basic sources and two basic kinds of new information. There is God, who gives truth without error. And there is the Evil One, who gives a distorted and erroneous "truth" through deception.

Meditation is the process of going to God and receiving truth for the situation at hand. (We will examine this further in chapter 13). Once we have received the truth, we then have the opportunity of choice. And choosing is usually done on the basis of the third capacity of the mind: reasoning.

The Capacity of Reason

Another capacity that God gave our minds is reasoning, calculating, coming to conclusions that are the basis for action. Again, we cannot choose whether or not we will reason, but only how and on what basis we will do so.

Let us consider the importance of reasoning that is revealed in its side effects and results: expectations, interpretations, and conclusions.

1. *Expectations.* Have you ever expected, presumed, or anticipated that something would happen? Whether or not you realized it at the time, you were using your capacity to reason. You considered the known facts, dipped into your reservoir of the subconscious, brought up a bucket of thoughts and feelings about the present situation — and arrived at certain expectations of what you figured

would happen. Then you could decide what you were going to do about it.

It is not wrong to have expectations. The Bible even has special words for certain expectations. It calls them "faith" and "hope." These are expectations based on the truth — the truth that comes from God.

During a two-week period, four of our church families received similar news about relatives of approximately the same age: an elderly parent had inoperable lung cancer. The diagnosis was "oat cell carcinoma," and it was spreading rapidly.

The prognosis was the same for all: possibly three months to live.

Three of the families were praying "healing" and "life." The other . . . well, I'll let her tell you herself. She says:

> The surgeon thought perhaps my mother would have three months. We began to ask our Father what we could pray for her. Our pastor had taught us that all prayer begins in the heart of the Father. Find out what is being done in heaven and pray for that on earth — get in agreement with the Father.
>
> But there was only silence. I received no answer. Words cannot describe the desolation, blackness, and pain I felt. The child-heart within me said to beg and plead for healing.
>
> After about three weeks the Lord said, "My child, pray that her body will receive the chemotherapy and radiation treatments."
>
> More time went by.
>
> Then God said, "I have a high purpose in all of this. If I wanted her death, I could take her instantaneously in any one of a thousand ways. I'm going to do a mighty work."
>
> And he did. Mother lived for eighteen months — not well, but courageously.
>
> Tears come to my eyes and heart when I think of the gold mine those months were for me and all our family. We were all radically changed in that crucible. We had the opportunity to close Mother's house for her last six months and nurse her around the clock at the end.
>
> Because of the Lord's insight, his truth, we were not overcome by presumptions or false expectations.

The outward appearance was *death*. But God had planned a time of inner healing and rebuilding of relationships for this woman and her family. A higher purpose. A lasting work for eternity. Not patching up this "tent," but a new creation!

For the other three families, too, the apparent expectation was *death*. But they didn't have the right kind of fellowship with the Lord. When death came, they were overwhelmed for a long period of time.

There is nothing more harmful than false expectations, those that can never be fulfilled. But when we reason on the basis of false data or untruth, we come up with many false expectations, erroneous assumptions, unrealistic anticipations. Of course, we don't know that this is so until we discover that things have not worked out. Then we become filled with anger. Or disappointment. Or fear. Or hopelessness.

The natural tendency is to assume that someone else failed or is to blame. Then we become bitter. It never seems to occur to most of us that often the reason for "failure" is having faulty reasoning based on false and erroneous facts.

Sometimes a couple enters marriage with the unrealistic expectation that marriage will solve all their problems and that they will now find the "happiness" that so far has escaped them. It never seems to occur to them that often their original reasoning is incorrect, since it is based on false and erroneous facts and is the cause for failure.

At our daughter's wedding the following was printed on the program:

> We are constantly tempted to want more from people than they can give.
>
> If we relate to them with the supposition that they were able to fulfill our deepest needs, we will find ourselves increasingly frustrated.
>
> If we expect a friend or lover to be able to take away our deepest pain, and expect from him or her something that cannot be given by human beings, we will be quickly disillusioned.

2. *Interpretations.* How many times have you been misunderstood? Your words, your actions, or your lack of response were falsely interpreted by someone close to you. Remember how it hurt, or hurts even now?

Through reasoning, we arrive at certain interpretations of what we think we know and perceive. Sometimes these interpretations are not sound or accurate because the information we based them on is incorrect. Since we do not recognize our information as wrong, we are sure we are right in our understanding of the matter. It's obvious to *us*.

Let us look at two biblical examples.

(a) *Interpretation Through Reasoning Used Wrongly* — Mark 2:1–12:

When Jesus was getting ready to heal a paralytic, he declared, "My son, your sins are forgiven" (v. 5).

The Scriptures then record: "But there were some of the scribes sitting there and reasoning in their hearts, 'Why does this man speak that way? He is blaspheming; who can forgive sins but God alone?' And immediately Jesus, aware in His spirit that they were reasoning that way within themselves, said to them, 'Why are you reasoning about these things in your hearts?' " (vv. 6–8).

The scribes' conclusion was wrong because one of their facts was wrong. They did not recognize that Jesus was God and therefore had the right to forgive sin.

(b) *Proper Use of Reasoning and Interpretation* — Romans 4:17–21:

Abraham reasoned that no matter what the other facts in the situation were, he and Sarah would have a child because God said so. This is good reasoning (cf Heb 11:11). Paul tells us in his letter to the Romans:

> (As it is written, "A father of many nations have I made you [Abraham]") in the sight of Him whom he believed, *even* God, who gives life to the dead and calls into being that which does not exist. In hope against hope he believed, in order that he might become a father of many nations, according to that which had been spoken, "So shall your descendants be." And without becoming weak in faith he contemplated his own body, now as good as dead since he was about a hundred years old, and the deadness of Sarah's womb; yet, with respect to the promise of God, he did not waver in unbelief, but grew strong in faith, giving glory to God, and being fully assured that what He had promised, He was able also to perform (4:17–21).

If we were to write that equation out in a mathematical formula, it would look like this:

GOD'S PROMISE — Abraham's advanced age — Sarah's barren womb =
"We will have a child!" (Abraham's reasoning)

In this, and so many other of life's equations, the positive factor of God's truth and promises cancels out the negative elements and brings a correct interpretation to our reasoning.

3. *Conclusions.* We have no control over how we feel, how we act — our attitudes, and actions — except as they are determined by our thoughts. All these elements are irrevocably tied together.

But since we *do* have control over what we think, it is possible to control our attitudes and actions. If I can think true thoughts, I can have attitudes and actions that will be right. And it is in "thinking God's thoughts with him" that I am able to think true thoughts and come to the correct conclusions and actions.

We will discover how this is done as we look into the process of meditation in the next chapter.

God says to us,

"As a child has eyesight
but only by teaching and study
does he learn the art of reading

so likewise

what I do for you is
to train you to comprehend intelligently
that which you see in the Spirit....

"Let Me be your teacher
and guide you into how to interpret
the information that comes to you....

Know that as you serve Me
you shall have very definite need
of the information I will give you....

It will provide you
with a knowledge of dangers
and will give you insight
into the needs of people to whom you minister.

I will make
your words meaningful
to the individual
and your heart sensitive
to his needs." [1]

1. Frances J. Roberts, *Come Away, My Beloved* (Ojai, Calif.: King's Farspan, Inc., 1970), p. 31.

13

The Process of Meditation

Since this is a technical chapter — one designed to show you "how to" — it seems best to start with some definitions.

1. Meditation
    is listening to God.
    is thinking his thoughts with him.
    is the finding of his will and viewpoint.
    is the discovering of truth.
    is giving God a chance to speak.
2. Truth
    is the reality that lies behind appearance.
3. Appearance
    is the sensory impression or aspect of a thing that we perceive with our senses.
4. A Process
    is a method of doing something to arrive at a particular result or end; in this case, listening to what God has to say.
5. A Habit
    is a process that has been consciously and regularly repeated.
    is something we then do naturally and spontaneously without much conscious effort.

The Christian life is a life of doing God's will under the guidance of the Holy Spirit.

The child of God is forever facing a multitude of decisions —

mostly small, but sometimes of very great importance. Thus, to make decisions and live in God's will, the child of God must have a simple method of finding out and knowing God's will, of thinking God's thoughts with him.

This is what we have defined as "meditation" — thinking God's thoughts with him — but it cannot be understood by merely looking at the idea. Meditation has to be experienced by a person seeking to know God. It is a *process* consciously and consistently repeated until it becomes a habit. And the *habit* of meditation is essential to Christian living.

Understanding the Process of Meditation

We saw in the last chapter that what we feel and do is determined by what we think. We are now going to examine the process whereby we can know God's thoughts on a given matter — so that we can do what he wants us to do. Understanding our thought life helps us understand the process of meditation, which begins when our attention is focused on a problem, person, or condition.

Sometimes we choose what we are going to think about, what we will focus our attention on — watching a certain TV program, reading our Bible, or writing to a friend.

Other times we are forced by the circumstances of life to think about certain things, and the focus of our thoughts is usually not one that we would have chosen for ourselves. Our attention is drawn and held by the situation at hand — a rebellious child, an angry boss, or a bounced check.

However they come to us, the thoughts in our mind affect the way we live. They come from one of three places:

1. Through the five senses, the eye and the ear in particular. That is, we see or hear something in the physical world.
2. From the subconscious mind, our reservoir of remembered experiences.
3. From the spiritual world.

How can we determine whether these thoughts are true or false? How can we find the truth?

Here is a process that I pray will become a lifestyle for you, as it has for me. To help you understand the process you go through in meditation, let us set up a situation that might occur in real life, observe it, and then interpret it. We will stop at each point to check what we are doing.

Step 1   *The Object of Your Attention (The Fact/Situation that Focuses Your Mind)*

Meditation begins with what you are currently thinking about, whatever focuses your mind, the "object of your attention" at the moment.

For our set-up situation we will create a scenario in which your teenage daughter comes home two hours late. She was told to be in at midnight, but it is now 2:00 A.M. You have waited up for her, worrying about her. She becomes the "object of your attention" (Step 1).

There are some important facts we must observe about any "object of attention":

1. *We have a very limited view of any situation.* Regardless of how experienced or mature we may be, we "see" only the outward appearance. This is a sensory view, only what we perceive through our biological senses. It is not the whole picture.

Let us take a biblical example. When God sent Samuel to anoint a king for Israel to replace Saul, he instructed Samuel not to consider physical appearance (Saul was both tall and handsome but had sinned and been rejected): ". . . God *sees* not as man sees, for man looks at the outward appearance, but the Lord looks at the heart" (1 Sam. 16:7b).

God not only looks at the heart of a man; he sees beneath the outward appearance of circumstances and situation as well. Jesus said, "Do not judge according to appearance, but judge with righteous judgment" (John 7:24).

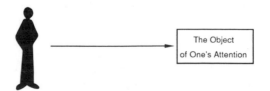

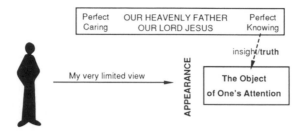

Trying to help the Corinthians understand that the outward view is not always God's perspective, Paul writes, "While we look not at the things which are seen, but at the things which are not seen . . ." (2 Cor. 4:18a).

2. *We are not able to properly interpret the situation.* Since our facts are obtained from our sensory view (what we see and hear and feel), the whole truth is simply not available to us.

In addition, we have the problem that the devil, the deceiver, is waiting to mislead and delude us. He takes our sensory perceptions and twists them to his purposes through our thought life. God tells us through John: "The great dragon was thrown down, the serpent of old who is called the devil and Satan, who deceives the whole world; he was thrown down to the earth, and his angels . . . with him (Rev. 12:9; cf. Rev. 20:2–3).

3. *We have a loving heavenly Father who has promised to lead us into "all truth."* That truth is the reality that lies behind appearances. In spite of our sensory or human shortcomings, meditation is possible because you and I as individuals hold certain fundamental beliefs built on the Scriptures. We also have the experience of obedience to God, and we have his Spirit of truth.

We have a loving heavenly Father who wants the very best for us, even as we do for our children. He wants to communicate with us and wants us to come to him. Our heavenly Father knows the *truth* about the "object of our attention." He has complete insight into the matter. He knows all about it, and what he knows is truth.

Jesus tells us: "But when He, the Spirit of truth, comes, He will guide you into all the truth; for He will not speak on his own initiative, but whatever He hears He will speak; and He will disclose to you what is to come" (John 16:13).

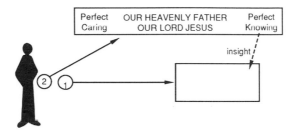

Step 1 in the meditation process then, involves focusing on the "object of attention" — remembering that *truth is the reality that lies beyond appearance.*

Step 2A *The Reasoning in Your Mind and the Actions that Result*

In our hypothetical situation, when the teenager comes in late, she appears to be okay. (If she were not okay, Step 2 would obviously be different.)

If you move from Step 1 to Step 2A after meeting her at the door, once you are assured she is okay, your anxiety turns to anger, frustration, and worry. You interpret your observation of her disobedient lateness by reasoning in your mind:

"What will she do next?"

"Will she get pregnant, like Jane down the street?"

"There is just no hope for her! This is the tenth time she's played a trick like this."

"I am a failure as a parent."

Your feelings of anger, frustration, and worry cause you to overreact, and you (a) falsely accuse the teenager, often making exaggerated statements; (b) punish inappropriately (too much, too late); (c) condemn yourself; (d) lose your cool (get angry); and/or (e) fight.

What alternative is there to these actions? The alternative is Step 2B. Instead of taking Step 2A (reasoning in your mind on the facts as you see them), you can move from Step 1 to alternate Step 2B.

Step 2B   *You Turn to God and Ask Him for Truth*

If you choose Step 2B, you have begun the meditation process. This is where you get God's point of view, his input, his truth, his love and care.

Meditation involves coming to our heavenly Father and our Lord Jesus to receive their outlook, their input, and their guidance on the matter at hand. Our confidence in asking God for his truth is based on Scriptures that are full of invitations to come to him for guidance, for help and encouragement. He has given us exhortations, commands, promises, and examples. Here are just a few of the great multitude of these Scriptures: Matthew 7:7–8; 2 Corinthians 1:3–4; Hebrews 4:15–16; James 1:5; 1 Peter 5:7.

Step 3   *You Stop Your Way of Thinking and Listen to (Hear) God's Truth*

This step involves allowing God to speak to us, and then reasoning on the basis of what *he* says. We stop our own way of thinking. We ask God what is the reality that lies behind the appearance.

In our set-up situation, God might say to you, "Your daughter is unsure of herself and is trying to be accepted by her friends."

God then would give you steps to take to build her confidence. "Spend more time with her," he might say to begin with. "Take her

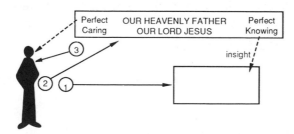

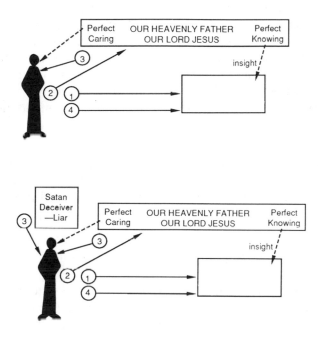

to lunch." Another time he might suggest, "Do things she enjoys doing. Love her and show her that God loves her. You then give her a foundation of love with which she can face the world."

Meditation continues as we listen to everything God has to say. He says it in our minds (thoughts), since the Holy Spirit lives inside of us to guide us into all truth. We learn to stop our train of thought — our way of thinking — and find out from God what we are supposed to do to use any situation redemptively. Then listening to what he says becomes habitual.

Step **Your Response: The Actions that Follow the Revelation**
4 **of His Truth**

Now comes that very important step: your response to God's insight and truth. You must give the appropriate response to what God says. It is not enough to hear him. You must respond in an appropriate way.

Meditation so far has involved facing a situation/person (Step 1); asking our heavenly Father for insight and truth (Step 2B); stopping your way of thinking and listening to God's truth (Step 3). The next step centers on your response to what he has shown you.

It is automatic in human thinking to reason out the things we observe. How we interpret these situations is the secret ingredient. As we have seen, there is a wrong way and the right way — God's way. Look again at the four steps in the process of meditation:

Step 1   — focusing our mind on a fact/situation

Step 2B — *not* trying to reason it out by ourselves (as in Step 2A), *nor* acting according to our own thought process, but asking our heavenly Father and our Lord Jesus for insight and truth

Step 3   — hearing his truth

Step 4   — responding to what God has shown us.

Remember, our confidence in asking God for his truth is based on Scriptures that are full of invitations to come to him for guidance, for help and encouragement. We have looked together at some of the exhortations, commands, promises, and examples he has given us. There are many more.

Let us consider again these three important facts:

1. God loves us as a father loves a child and wishes to commune with us.
2. God has sent his Spirit to live in us in order that this communion may take place.
3. God has given us "the mind of Christ" — the ability and capacity our Lord Jesus had on earth — to be able to communicate with the Father.

Looking objectively at our set-up situation, we realize how important it is to use the right reasoning process. There are scriptural truths that can help us, truths we need to recognize. The apostle Paul writes:

Now we have received, not the spirit of the world, but the Spirit who is from God, that we might know the things freely given to us by

God, which things we also speak, not in words taught by human wisdom, but in those taught by the Spirit, combining spiritual *thoughts* with spiritual *words*. But a natural man does not accept the things of the Spirit of God; for they are foolishness to him, and he cannot understand them ... (1 Cor. 2:12–14).

The Reality of Meditation

Faced with some situation, asking for insight and truth from God — and getting it? Yes, this is what he has promised his children.

We looked at a simple hypothetical situation to enable us to understand the principles of meditation. (It is very similar to something that really happened in one of my church families.) We will now examine real-life Situation A: *The "Rebellious" Teenager*, applying the four steps of meditation to its resolution.

Step 1   *The Object of Their Attention (The Fact/Situation that Focused Their Minds)*

This couple's sixteen-year-old daughter — we'll call her Mary — was giving her family fits. The parents would give Mary permission to go to the mall or a fast-food place. Later they would find out that she had gone other places — not bad places, just places that they had not actually given her permission to visit. They were concerned parents.

Step 2A   *The Reasonings in Their Minds and the Actions that Resulted*

The parents accused Mary of being rebellious and "grounded" her for a month. Mary couldn't understand why they were accusing and punishing her, when she had done nothing wrong. She became resentful. A real problem was developing in this family, but finally Mary's parents realized there was a better way. . . .

Step 2B   *The Parents Asked the Lord for Truth and Help*

Step   **They Stopped Their Way of Thinking and Listened to**
3   **(Heard) God's Truth**

In a flash of insight, God revealed the problem to these parents.
The Lord said that in their reasoning they were wrongly interpreting
all the symptoms as "rebellion." So, they were treating everything
their daughter did as rebellion.

The Lord said that Mary was not rebellious but had not been
properly trained. During her childhood, Mary had trooped from
house to house with her neighborhood friends. Since her parents
knew she was safe then, they never requested that, for her own
safety, she was to check in with them before going from one place
to another.

Later on, when Mary got her driver's license, she began to learn
this part of the family's house rules. But she didn't understand that
her much greater mobility really added a drastic new dimension to
the fact that she must check in with her parents about her
movements.

WARNING: If we do not turn to the Lord for help, we are in danger
of receiving information from one or two other places:

(a) *From ourselves.* Through "leaning to our own understanding,"
we can come up with wrong and distorted conclusions due to our
lack of all the relevant facts.

(b) *From the Evil One.* The deceiver stands ready to "aid" us by
distorting the truth. The surest protection is to go to our Lord, who
has promised to guide us into all truth.

Since our Father has promised to answer, we can by faith expect
an answer. We will receive it. He loves us too much to ignore us,
and he is faithful to his promise that he will answer. The answer
might not be what we expect to hear or what we want to hear, but
he will answer.

Step   **Their Response: The Actions that Followed the**
4   **Revelation of His Truth**

After Mary's parents heard from the Lord, they talked with her,
explaining how they knew from God's revelation that she was not
rebellious. Tears coursed down Mary's cheeks as she was freed from
false condemnation and guilt.

Her parents explained the new rules and the reasons behind them. They asked her cooperation and got it. The problem was solved.

Note: This last step — Response to God's revelation of truth — is vital in the meditation and listening process. We must respond to God in an appropriate way. Our response is our faith walk. We are walking by what he says, rather than by how we interpret what we see or perceive with our senses.

Conclusion: Looking back, we can see how a normally obedient child was being made into a rebel because of the misinterpretation of the situation by her parents.

To help you understand more clearly, let us walk together through real-life situation B: *The "Self-Willed" Child*. This time, the scenario involves my own daughter. With Susan's permission, my wife, Johnnie, tells the story.

Step 1   *The Object of Johnnie's Attention*

"Though Susan was still in junior high school, her weight had blossomed out of control. She didn't fit my idea of what a young lady should look like.

"I'd tried so hard to train her to be neat and feminine. I'd remind her to keep her notebooks straight, take better care of her clothes and hair, and cut down on her eating. But nothing seemed to work.

"Susan gave us the impression she didn't care what people thought about her."

Step 2A   *The Reasonings in Johnnie's Mind and the Actions that Resulted*

"But I cared," Johnnie says. "I cared deeply. And I didn't know what to do. I wondered how I should pray for Susan. Should I ask God to remove her strong self-will?"

Step 2B   *Johnnie Asked the Lord for Truth and Help*

"I went before the Lord. I asked him to show me what was wrong with Susan."

Step   *Johnnie Stops Her Way of Thinking and Listens to*
3   *(Hears) God's Truth*

"As I prayed, God showed me the problem with Susan was, first of all, myself. I had too much pride about what other people thought when they saw Susan. And pride is sin. He also wanted me to stop correcting Susan with a critical spirit, calling it 'my duty to train her.'

"Once again, I surrendered Susan to the Lord that afternoon. 'Lord,' I prayed, 'she's yours. I'll get out of the way and let you work. Now, please show me how to pray for her.'

"The Lord seemed to say to me, 'Johnnie, if you'll let me, I'll show you why Susan is acting this way. You aren't seeing into the windows of her heart, Johnnie.'

"I knew I was reacting to *what* Susan was doing, but I hadn't thought about *why* she was doing it. I spent a lot of time in prayer about Susan over those next few days.

"One morning, the Lord showed me that Susan didn't think we loved her as much as we did Richard, her older brother. That seemed absurd to me. 'It isn't true, Lord,' I argued. 'You *know* Peter and I love Susan as much as we love Richard!'

"So very gently the Lord answered, 'Yes, I know. But *Susan* doesn't know it.'

"Now I could understand *why* she was creating problems at school and at home. Unconsciously clamoring for attention, Susan just didn't believe we loved her as much as we loved her happy-go-lucky brother, Richard, who's just thirteen months older than she. Of course we love her as much! But if she didn't think so, we had a real problem.

"After I got over that low blow, I really began to pray. I asked God to show me specific ways I could communicate love to Susan. I also asked him to teach Susan how to respond to love. I realized this would have to be a two-way affair.

"During my early-morning prayer time, it seemed as though the Lord was dropping little thoughts to me on how to love Susan: 'Don't go grocery shopping until Susan comes in from school and can go with you.' 'Don't buy any more clothes for Susan until she can help select them.' 'Let Susan help you cook supper tonight, choosing her favorite foods.'

"They seemed to be such little insignificant things to do!"

Step   **Johnnie's Response: The Actions that Followed the**
4   **Revelation of His Truth**

"I completely rearranged my schedule to be available to do things with Susan and for her. At first she was suspicious. But, as I continued, there was a softening in Susan.

"God had been true to his word. He had let me look intently through the window of her heart and see what the root of Susan's problem was. I saw that he didn't take away her self-will; he just converted it into what he had put it there for in the first place."

As a family we thank the Lord for what Johnnie and Susan learned through that experience. And I trust it will be helpful to you, too, as you relate to your family and friends.

Now let me show you how the four steps of the meditation process can work in your daily quiet time, by sharing a page from what I will call Situation C: My Quiet Time and Reading a Bible Passage.

Step   **The Object of My Attention**
1

In this case, it was Hebrews 1:13 that focused my mind: "But to which of the angels has He ever said, 'Sit at My right hand, until I make Thine enemies a footstool for Thy feet'?"

Step   **The Reasonings in My Mind and the Actions that**
2A   **Resulted**

I said to myself, "I can't understand what this verse has to do with me — today. I don't even know why it is in the Bible, except as it has to do with Jesus — and that's a long way ahead in the future. I think I'll skip it."

But I didn't skip it. I asked the Lord about it instead....

Step
2B
Asking the Lord for Truth and Help

My prayer was: "Lord, would you mind explaining the relevance of this to me for my life *now*?"

Step
3
Listening to (Hearing) His Truth

This is the answer God gave me on May 19, 1986, about that Scripture:

"Peter, my Son Jesus is seated at my right hand, and you are raised up and seated with him (cf. Eph. 2:6). You have the privilege of sitting there with us (cf. 1 John 1:3). This is where your heart needs to be continually — seated in fellowship with me.

"Your trouble is that you are running around trying to take care of your troubles, your 'enemies,' and I have to use my right hand to get you to sit down.

"If you would sit and fellowship with us, you would set my right hand free to make your enemies your footstool. Come, my son, sit and fellowship with us, and we will take care of your enemies. Notice, you have not done too well at doing it yourself!"

Step
4
My Response to His Truth

My part in "thinking God's thoughts" is responding *now*. "Lord, please forgive me for my impatience and self-sufficiency. Teach me to sit in confidence at your right hand knowing that you will make my enemies — my troubles — my footstool."

Making These Experiences *Yours*

Such real-life experiences of others are good for them and even may be exciting. But each of us wants to know how to make these experiences our own.

How do you know God's voice? How can you tell what thoughts are from yourself, from the devil, or from God?

You know God's voice because you know God. You know how he acts, how he thinks, what he wants. You recognize his voice because you know him, and you remember that Jesus mentioned the shepherd, "and the sheep follow him because they know his voice" and referred to himself, "I am the good shepherd; and I know My own, and My own know Me" (John 10:4, 14).

We have looked at the four ways to recognize God's voice: by the *approach* he makes, by the *relevance* of what he says, by the *content* of what he says, and by the *results* his words produce in us.

This is what meditation is all about.

My prayer is that soon — today! — you will begin to put the four steps of meditation into practice and that you will begin to know God better.

> No new truth can be generated
> in the midst of activity.
>
> New life
> springs from the placid pools of reflection.
>   Quiet meditation
>   and deep worship
>   are a prerequisite
>   if you are to receive my words
>   and comprehend my thoughts.
>
> Some graces of the soul
> are gained in motion.
>
>   Faith may be developed in action.
>   Endurance in the midst of storms and turmoil.
>   Courage may come in the front lines of battle.
>
> But wisdom
> and understanding
> and revelation
>   unfold as dew forms on the petals of a rose
>   — in quietness.
>
> Did not Jesus learn from his Father
> through the silences
> of lonely nights on the mountain?

Shall I not teach you likewise?

Will you, my child, set aside for me
these hours for lonely vigil
that I may have the opportunity
to minister to you?

The inner way,
the way of meditation,
is dangerous.
Any practice which
brings us into contact
with forces from the
spiritual world
in this way
puts us into the middle
of a mighty struggle.

To enter this arena
for curiosity
or diversion
can be disastrous. [1]

1. Morton Kelsey, *The Other Side Of Silence* (New York, Paulist Press, 1976), p. 40.

14

The Dangers in Meditation

There are dangers, in fact, grave dangers, in meditation. The tremendous positive possibilities of life resulting from a continuing encounter with our living Lord can be threatened by the great negative possibilities of deception.

Paul alerts us that Satan disguises himself as an angel of light (2 Cor. 11:13).

John the Beloved forewarns all generations of believers, "Beloved, do not believe every spirit, but test the spirits to see whether they are from God; because many false prophets have gone out into the world" (1 John 4:1).

Explaining how to do this "testing" John says, "By this you know the Spirit of God: every spirit that confesses that Jesus Christ has come in the flesh is from God; and every spirit that does not confess Jesus is not from God; and this is the spirit of the antichrist, of which you have heard that it is coming" (1 John 4:1–3).

John further narrows the "test." What he says next would sound super-egotistical if his words were not divinely inspired: "We are from God; he who knows God listens to us; he who is not from God does not listen to us. By this we know the spirit of truth and the spirit of error" (1 John 4:6).

Although the dangers are great, Paul doesn't want us to be scaredy-cats. "God has not given us a spirit of fear," he reminds Timothy, "but of power and love and discipline" (2 Tim. 1:7). Just before he finishes his letter to the Ephesian church, Paul admonishes:

Finally, be strong in the Lord, and in the strength of His might.

Put on the full armor of God, that you may be able to stand firm against the schemes of the devil. For our struggle is not against flesh and blood, but against the rulers, against the powers, against the world forces of this darkness, against the spiritual forces of wickedness in the heavenly places.

Therefore, take up the full armor of God, that you may be able to resist in the evil day, and having done everything, to stand firm (Eph. 6:10–13).

The Danger of Seeking "To Use" God

The primary function of meditation is to have fellowship with God. Never forget this and never get far from it. But the plan of the enemy and the tendency of unregenerative flesh is to "use" God:

for ego exaltation

for successful ministry

for personal gain

for one's own ends

We would rather "use God" than to be used of God for his created and redemptive purpose: to have fellowship with us. Out of that fellowship we glorify him on earth.

How to Avoid this Danger

If God gave you nothing but himself, would you be satisfied? The answer reveals whether you are loving God for himself, or for what you hope he will do for you.

When you find yourself no longer just enjoying the presence of God,

When you find your prayers are limited to asking for things for yourself,

When you are in a hurry to get answers for your needs,

When Christian ministry becomes the all-important thing in your life,

Then there is the subtle danger that you are using God for your ends.

To put it simply, when you are no longer enjoying God for himself, then you are missing the primary function of meditation.

The Danger of Anything Outside the Boundary of Biblical Revelation

The Bible contains a record of God and his dealings with man. In it there is a clear revelation of God, his character, his ways, his will, and his commands. God's principles are consistently portrayed and clearly spelled out: We must forgive as we have been forgiven. We must love our enemies and not seek revenge. It is wrong to steal. It is wrong to judge others.

The Holy Spirit will never guide us to do things that are outside the boundary lines of biblical revelation: things inconsistent with the character of God; things divergent to his ordained ways; things inconsistent with his explicit command.

For example, the Scriptures clearly teach that it is not our business to judge others. Jesus said, "Do not judge lest you be judged" (Matt. 7:1). Paul, writing to the Romans, admonishes, "Therefore let us not judge one another anymore, but rather determine this — not to put an obstacle or a stumbling block in a brother's way" (Rom. 14:13). This does not mean that we have to be naive. Rather, it means that we are not to pass judgment, to declare others guilty, and proceed to punish them in some form.

It is common among Christians to judge others because of some perceived or actual doctrinal deviation. This is the way it is usually done:

1. We declare them guilty.
2. We proceed to pronounce judgment by labeling them as "fundamentalist" or "liberal."

3. We determine the punishment deserved, which could be condemnation or refusal to have fellowship with them in a specific way.

The Holy Spirit will never lead us to judge another person — not
even for the "good" reason of getting others to pray about it. The
evil one can make the procedure seem so right, even spiritual. He
will supply abundant rational justification. Satan is a wily, professional debater and can easily convince us that the end justifies the
means. We in our own strength could be overwhelmed quickly by
his tactics.

If we know the Scriptures, we will immediately know Satan's voice
is not our shepherd's voice. It is abundantly clear that the God who
says "do not judge" will not lead us to do so.

How to Avoid this Danger

1. Have an ever-increasing knowledge of God himself. He never
   does anything contrary to his word or his nature.
2. When in doubt, *don't*. Check your judgment with other believers, especially those that God has given you for your fulfill-
   ment and watchcare: your partner, your pastor, your
   undershepherd.
3. Know the subtle traps that Satan uses to get believers to step
   across the line. Avoid them. Paul says, "we are not ignorant
   of his schemes" (2 Cor. 2:11).

The Danger of Knowledge Without Application

One of the strongest statements in Scripture about this danger
was penned by the apostle Paul to the Corinthians, "knowledge
makes arrogant, but love edifies" (1 Cor. 8:1b).

As surely as Satan tempted Eve to eat of the tree of knowledge,
so he also tempts us. We are in great danger of substituting knowledge for love. Love is obeying our Father's commands. Whenever
we obey him, we are edified. We are built up. By our own experience
we *know* the truth. Knowledge is knowing facts. Knowledge tends to
make us proud; often it is the substitute for obedience.

Merton Kelsey reaches back into Christian history to make this point:

> Out of the literature of prayer, Christmas Humphreys passes on to us this counsel: "Unless each step in inner growth finds corresponding expression in *service to mankind* the student treads a dangerous path, and works in vain."[1]

An example of this danger might be the believer who knows that marriage relationships are under direct attack today. Satan's approach could well be to read another book, listen to another tape, attend another conference, learn how to be a better partner or parent.

Our Lord's approach will always be to "flesh out" what we already know, what he has shown us in the past. Many times we do not need to know anything more; we need to put into practice what we already know. James warns us, "To one who knows the right thing to do, and does not do it, to him it is sin" (James 4:17). This concept can be humbling, but it is God's way and leads to victory.

How to Avoid this Danger

Be more concerned about personal obedience than about knowledge. Keep asking him, "Lord, is my obedience up to date?"

The Danger of Hearing God for Others

As one listens to the Lord and gains confidence through experienced communication with him, it is easy to become overconfident. It is at this point that the enemy begins to slip in words about "God's will" for other people.

The "God told me to tell you . . ." syndrome has done more damage than can be described here. Of course, the enemy will let it work some of the time but usually he is setting up both you and the other party for a big fall. Both parties are usually hurt. But the worst damage is the discredit to the name of God and the resultant

1. Morton Kelsey, *The Other Side Of Silence* (New York, Paulist Press, 1976), p. 116.

suspicion with which communion with God is regarded. Those who declare God does speak to man are considered religious freaks.

Great damage has been done when one "hears from God" in these areas:

physical illness and getting well

God's will for others: for their lives, their business, their personal life

how others ought to act and things they "ought to" give up

the sins of other people.

It is not that God never speaks about such matters. It is that we as his children must be extremely careful, realizing how many times Satan has been able to discredit our Lord through our well-meaning interference in others' lives.

Here is only one example of this danger. A pastor and his wife had a critically sick child. They requested the prayers of people, several of whom were well-known. Over and over again they were assured that the Lord had said the child would be healed. But the child died in his mother's arms at a prayer meeting. I do not need to tell of the devastation done by such false hope.

How to Avoid this Danger

1. Remember that God can and wants to tell people personally what his will is for them. Sometimes people cop-out on their responsibility of going to him for themselves and are like the children of Israel who wanted Moses to hear God for them and tell them what to do. "Speak to us yourself and we will listen; but let not God speak to us . . ." (Exod. 20:19).
2. Remember that when God speaks to you about or for others, it is usually a *confirming word* concerning something he has already told them. God is confirming through you that they heard correctly.
3. Remember to check carefully if you have a word (other than encouragement!) for someone and be cautious when you give it.

   Recently a man I am discipling asked me, "Pastor, should I quit smoking?"

"I really do not know. Why don't you ask the Lord?" I an-swered, deliberately pushing him into the Lord, because I want to teach him dependence on the Lord. Obviously, I will not always be around, but the Lord will. I am not always right, but the Lord is.

4. All this is not to say that God does not speak to us about others, rather, thoughts that come to us from God about others are usually for the purpose of intercession. Oswald Chambers makes that clear when he says,

> The revelation is made to us not through the acuteness of our minds, but by the direct penetration of the Spirit of God.
>
> One of the subtlest burdens God ever puts on us as saints is this burden of discernment concerning other souls. He reveals things in order that we may take the burden of these souls before Him and form the mind of Christ about them, and as we intercede on His line, God says He will give us 'life for them that sin not unto death.'[2]

We can always pray for those God brings to our minds but we need to be careful about speaking "his word" to them.

The Danger of Hearing God in Big Things

"Big things" are those things that involve other people: *their* re-sources of time, talents, and money. Unfortunately, too many saints spend their energies on dead works, projects that do not build up the kingdom of God.

These projects are usually started by strong leaders who get "a word from God" for a large group of people who never question God for themselves, but take for granted the "word" was from God.

For example, our church has two Sunday morning services. It would be nice to hold only one. To do so, we would have to build a much larger auditorium at a great cost. On the basis of a word from God to me alone, I would be careful about building a larger auditorium. Caution here would mean that many other leaders in our fellowship would hear the same word from God on this matter.

2. Oswald Chambers, *My Utmost for His Highest*, March 31, p. 91.

How to Avoid this Danger

1. When others are going to be affected by your decision, give them an opportunity to hear from God.
2. When there is not unity among the leaders (church or family), it must be regarded as a caution signal to wait and seek God further until a basic unity surfaces.
3. Respect what God says through others who are involved, for each of us is vulnerable in making mistakes. (Mistakes that affect only the pray-er are one thing; those that affect other people are another matter.)

The Danger of Seeking to Put Your Guidance onto Others

When God leads an individual into some pattern of behavior, prohibition, or call of ministry, it is unwise (and wrong) for him or her to assume that God wants everyone around to do exactly the same thing.

There are factors in God's revelation that are dependent on an individual's maturity, spiritual gifting, God's special calling, God's testings. Since God makes each of us unique, his revelation to us will most likely be different from his revelation to other persons.

But, where God guides, God blesses — and it is easy for any of us to think God wants the same thing for others.

For example, God leads a person to stop smoking. When God leads, he helps. And so the individual is able to stop. Victory!

When we gain victory in any area, we talk about it, testify to it. We easily attach to that testimony something like this: "Everybody can do it — and everybody ought to do it *now*! I quit smoking and you can, too. God will help you."

We forget that we were able to quit because God guided us to do so, because he answered and helped. We forget that our liberty can be bondage to other people and bring them into condemnation, unless God speaks to them, too.

How to Avoid this Danger

1. Remember that what God says to you is *for you*.
2. Be cautious when testifying about it, until God releases you

to do so. God told my friend, Jamie Buckingham, to say nothing about his weight loss until he had maintained it for a year.
3. When you do testify about your victory, avoid putting anyone else under condemnation.

The Danger of Letting What God Says to You Be Eternal

We jokingly say that "eternal life" is anything that is started in a Baptist church—meaning that once a thing is started, it never can be stopped because we assume God wants it forever. This is an insidious danger.

We pass through many phases of life and service in our spiritual growth. God sometimes speaks to us about patterns of behavior, types of ministry, or modes of operation that are peculiarly fitted to our circumstances at that particular moment.

Of course, when we obey we are blessed. But we must remember that blessings come because *of obedience* and not because of a particular procedure or behavior. But one of the subtle plans of the enemy is to get us to associate blessings with behavior and patterns of behavior rather than obedience to God.

My experience with our Lord is that when I begin to associate blessings with behavior rather than with him, he ceases to bless that behavior. Then I come back and discover that *he, and not my behavior, is the source of all blessings.*

As we mature the Lord Jesus moves us to new levels of behavior, new ways of doing things in a more mature way. The way I conduct my personal devotions, for example, has changed many times over the years. At each level my devotional format was enriching and I felt blessed. I was tempted to stay in that familiar pattern. Often to get my attention, our Lord would dry up that well and move me into a different way of fellowship with Him.

When I followed a new pattern, many things changed: the length of time, the procedure followed, the emphasis given. My latest encounter has been in "Beholding the Lord." This pattern has less Scripture, less asking. More listening, more worship.

How to Avoid this Danger

1. Remember each new level of maturity will demand new levels of behavior.

2. Remember that the Lord wants to keep you attached to him, *not to his ways*; so his guidance will often involve change.
3. When the pattern you follow seems to be monotonous and dry, check to see if the Lord is leading you to a new device.

The Danger of Neglecting God's Ordained Channels of Authority

It is obvious that God has chosen certain channels of authority in various areas of life. In the home, the channel is the parents. In society, it is government officials. At work, it is the boss. In the church, it is the leaders.

Part of our old nature rebels at authority. One of the evidences of sin is that every man does what is right in his own eyes (Deut. 12:8). "All of us like sheep have gone astray," says Isaiah. "Each of us has turned to his own way" (Isa. 53:6). Our own way may be good or bad — but it is *our own*! And each of us is determined to have "my own way."

One of the ways God protects us (and therefore speaks to us) is through channels of authority. To neglect to consult authorities, to hear from them, to seek their advice, is dangerous. Paul calls authorities "a minister of God to you for good" (Rom. 13:4).

How to Avoid this Danger

1. Recognize God-given authorities as *God-given*. Seek their advice. Listen to their instruction and counsel. See them as a channel God uses to speak to you.
2. Recognize your tendency to want to do your own thing. See your authorities as one of God's checks.
3. Recognize that God holds you responsible to hear and obey your authorities. (Of course, when morality is involved, then disobedience must be done with great respect. Note the respect the apostles Paul and Peter had for authorities who were wicked.)
4. Recognize that God uses authorities to conform you to his image; that all authorities are under his authority and he can change them or change their hearts at will. *Jesus is Lord.*

The Danger of Being too Dogmatic

Satan greatly encourages one of our tendencies. Having heard from our Lord and seeing his message work out, we become dogmatic. Sometimes that assurance pushes us to the place of dogmatism, expressed not only in *what* we say but in *how* we say it. "God told me — and no matter what you or anybody else says, I know I am right!"

When we need to share what God has told us, it should be done with humility and caution, with this kind of attitude: "I believe the Lord Jesus is asking me to share this with you. I hope you will pray about it and see if you get a message that agrees with this."

There is an unpretentiousness to this attitude, room for the possibility of error, coupled with caution and humility. May God help us to "have this attitude in ourselves which was also in Christ Jesus" (Phil. 2:5).

How to Avoid this Danger

1. Recognize that Satan is an angel of light.
2. Recognize the possibility that you might be mistaken.
3. Move cautiously and allow the Lord time to correct your mistakes.

At the beginning of this chapter I warned about the dangers in meditation. If there were a way to install a flashing red light here, I would do so. To enter the spiritual world without understanding the inherent dangers present there, could lead to confusion, disillusionment, and even destruction. It is imperative that you read and heed these warnings in your pilgrimage to the inner world of meditation.

However, fear of the dangers should not keep us from this inner journey. Rather, since so many Christians have experienced these dangers, we should be cautious "in order that no advantage be taken of us by Satan; for we are not ignorant of his schemes" (2 Cor. 2:11).

Morton Kelsey explains:

> Indeed there is only one thing more dangerous than entering upon this way [of meditation], and that is *not* entering it (assuming you have a developed ego), for you then allow the destructive forces

free play. If you do not get into the battle yourself and try to stay in touch with the forces of light you become a blind target. You allow the forces of destructiveness to enter and eat away at your own soul.[3]

Let me encourage you with the tremendous positive possibilities of life in a continuing encounter with our living Lord!

3. Morton Kelsey, *The Other Side Of Silence* (New York, Paulist Press, 1976), p. 40.

5

Fellowshiping with God Through Hearing His Voice

The Scripture said: Do not forsake the works of thy hands! (Ps.
    138:8).

My soul said: Father, what does this mean for me now?

My Father said:

My child,
    I have invested too much in you
    to forsake you.

You
    are the object
    of my creative and redemptive plan.

It is for fellowship with me
that I designed you
    that I created you
    that I reclaimed you.

When I sent my son into this world
    it was to demonstrate to you
    the possibility of fellowship with me
        where you are
    as well as to make fellowship possible
    by taking care of the sin that prevented it.

As you read the Scriptures
    do you not see that my Son Jesus and I
    always had fellowship together?

That is why
   when he bore your sins and I had to forsake him
      he suffered such agony.
Would it have been agony if he had been used to
not having fellowship with me?

No.

In eternity he had fellowship with me.

In a human body on earth
   amongst people and conditions like you live in
   he had fellowship with me
      — AND SO CAN YOU!

No.
I will not forsake you.

More than that,
I will finish and perfect
   what I have called you for
both as an individual and as part of my bride.

Your need is not to be concerned about me forsaking you
but your being too preoccupied and forsaking me.

15

Hearing God in Scripture Reading

The best and easiest place to fellowship with God is in the Scriptures....

Psalm 60:8

For years it has been my practice to read through the Book of Psalms every month. Inevitably, when I came to Psalm 60, I would skip verse 8: "Moab is my washpot" (KJV). Since the same words also appear in Psalm 108:9, I skipped the passage at least twenty-four times a year.

I had never heard a sermon on it. Never seen it on a Scripture plaque. Never learned it in any Scripture memory system. But it was important enough for God to include *twice* in the Psalms!

Have you noticed this verse before? Do you know what it means?

One day in my fellowship time with God, I came to this verse and, as usual, started to skip over it.

God said, "Stop, Peter! Get your Bible dictionary and look up 'Moab.'" There I discovered that the Moabites were Israel's wicked relatives who lived right next door!

Then the Lord Jesus Christ said to me, "The meaning of this Scripture is this: When my people Israel got dirty, I used their wicked relatives as a 'washpot' to clean them up."

It was interesting to discover the meaning of this verse, but it seemed totally irrelevant to my own life.

"Lord," I asked, "what does a 2,700-year-old Scripture about Israel and Moab have to do with me?"

Then the Lord said, "Now here is the interpretation for you, Peter. You have been praying for me to change your son John. Every day you give me a list of the things you want me to do in him. Now you need to see this from my perspective. You need to understand what I want and what I am doing. I am using the behavior of your child to speak to you, to get your attention. I want to clean *you* up."

The focus of my prayers changed after hearing God's words on this Scripture. I began to ask God to do his work in me, to clean me up — instead of asking him to change John. And oh! the living lessons God is working in me through this child!

You see how vastly different meditating on Scripture is from studying Scripture! Both are important, and the sincere, earnest Christian cannot afford to neglect either.

Psalm 118:25

On another occasion, the Holy Spirit stopped me at Psalm 118:25: "O Lord, do save we beseech Thee, do send prosperity."

"Do you want prosperity," he asked me, "from my point of view and by my standards of evaluation or from yours? Do you want prosperity based on time and materialism or on eternity and eternal values?"

After giving me time to consider his question a moment, the Lord continued: "My child, do you know how I would answer such a prayer from my point of view? Suppose, to give my kind of prosperity, I had to take away the world's kind of prosperity, would you still want it?

"To the people of this world, prosperity is almost always money and the things it can buy. Having those things that make life easier, more comfortable, more enjoyable, and more useful. In my world, the kingdom of heaven on earth, it is far different.

"Prosperity," God said to me, "is a pure heart. It's a seeing eye for spiritual things. A listening ear. A strong faith. Full love. A real hope. Above all, prosperity means a genuine fellowship with me. It means really helping others to come to me and trust me.

"Do you still want to pray this prayer?" God asked.

I was silent, thinking over what God had said. I questioned my own fearful heart. And my gracious, all-knowing God spoke again.

"Oh, yes" he said, "I will give you what you need to survive in this world. But for you — and for most of my people — it means *not* being wealthy. You cannot and will not be wealthy or successful in the eyes of this world. Well, Peter? Still want to pray this prayer?"

Now, What About You?

If you have never read the Scriptures while letting the Holy Spirit teach you as you read, you are in for the greatest and most profitable time of your life.

At best, all commentaries and devotional books are second best. They are what God said to somebody else. They are good and profitable, but in no way to be compared with what he says to you personally.

Let us look at what will happen when you let God teach you. He will make the Scriptures come alive as he interprets them, as he applies them, as he makes them relevant to where you are right now.

You will experience (1) *revelation* (God will tell you about himself); (2) *interpretation* (what the Scriptures really mean); and (3) *application* (how the Scriptures are relevant in your life right now).

Revelation

The disciples were discussing rather generally what the people were saying about Jesus, when he made it personal: "But whom do you say that I am?" (Matt. 16:15).

Jesus' question to Simon Peter was answered with this statement: "Thou art the Christ, the Son of the living God" (v. 16).

To this Jesus said, ". . . flesh and blood [people] did not reveal this to you, but My Father who is in heaven!" (v. 17).

Revelation occurs when our God reveals himself to us so that we too can say, "I know whom I have believed, and I am convinced that he is able to guard what I have entrusted to him until that day" (2 Tim. 1:12b).

There is nothing more important in your Christian walk than your personal knowledge and understanding of God.

How about apple pie? Does God like apple pie? If I think he does, I will make apple pies for him!

I will try to find new exciting recipes to provide variety, attempting to please his taste for apple pie. I will want to become an expert on apple pies, so he and I can converse about them.

I will import-apples, do studies on which apples are the best, sweetest, most juicy. I will seek different kinds of flour and other special ingredients, trying to make the best apple pie possible. *Wouldn't you do the same, if you thought God likes apple pie?*

Why is it important to know what God likes?

Religion is nothing more than man's responding to the God he knows or thinks he knows. A wrong God-concept brings a wrong response; an inadequate concept of God brings an inadequate response — hence, an inadequate religion.

A maturing concept of God results in a maturing response and thereby a proper response to God. God desires to reveal himself to us personally, and he will do this as we are able to receive and willing to receive. The greater the knowledge of God, the greater the fellowship.

I have far greater fellowship with my older son than with my younger son, partly because the older son has had more years to know me and therefore is able to respond more appropriately to his knowledge of what I am like. The degree of fellowship is in direct proportion to the amount of personal knowledge one has of the other person — and, of course, to the quality of the relationship as well.

Hebrews 3:10. The Father revealed himself to me one day when I was meditating on the Holy Spirit's words in Hebrews 3:10: ". . . and they did not know my ways."

God said, "My child, you must get to know my ways. If you only see and experience my works and do not understand my ways, you will act exactly like the children of Israel acted in the wilderness. They wouldn't trust me when they didn't like what I was doing. And they complained and rebelled.

"Let me tell you more about my ways. About the way I work and have decided to do business. My ways are determined by my sovereignty and fatherhood. I am God. I am in charge. I am responsible and I have responsibility. My sovereignty means that I have knowl-

edge and wisdom, and my fatherhood means that I am vitally con-
nected with and care for my children.

"I know what's coming up and how it will affect you and your
behavior. So, in my sovereignty and knowledge, I do those things
that are best for you. As the knowledgeable Father, I see the future
and want you to prepare for it, so I plan my ways according to this.

"My sovereignty and fatherhood mean not only knowledge and
power, but also goodness. I am sovereign in goodness, and my
ways are good. 'Good' in the ultimate sense of the word, whether
or not you can see it from your viewpoint.

"Understand, my child, that my ways are determined by my tim-
ing and not by your comprehension of time. My ways are sover-
eignly viewed, from sovereign knowledge, power, and goodness.
Why would you rebel and refuse when all I have in mind is for your
best? Accept my sovereignty, my Lordship. Accept my ways.

"Another thing about my way, Peter, is that it is the way of *praise*.
If you believe my sovereign knowledge, power, and goodness —
really believe this — then you will demonstrate it by praise.

"You will praise me, for you know I am causing all things to work
together for good as you walk in my ways. You will praise me in all
things and at all times if you believe in my sovereignty."

As a result of the Father's communication with me, I could see
the inconsistency in my own life.

I answered him, "Lord, I do proclaim that you are sovereign.
Altogether wise. Powerful, able to do all. And good, always concerned with our ultimate welfare. And yet, with the same lips, I
grumble and complain and express unbelief rather than praise.

"Lord, may I be consistent as you said, in all things and at all
times, because I believe you and trust you."

His *love in me*? One morning in my quiet time Jesus asked me,
"How do you know you have my love in you? (1 John 2:5). Do you
know how to tell the difference?

> We know that we have passed out of death into life, because we
> love the brethren. He who does not love abides in death.
> Beloved, let us love one another, for love is from God; and every
> one who loves is born of God and knows God. . . . And we have come
> to know and have believed the love which God has for us. God is
> love, and the one who abides in love abides in God, and God abides
> in him.
> We love, because He first loved us. If some one says, 'I love God,'

and hates his brother, he is a liar; for the one who does not love his brother whom he has seen, cannot love God whom he has not seen. And this commandment we have from Him, that the one who loves God should love his brother also (1 John 3:14; 4:7, 16, 19–21).

Can you see from these three examples how God delights in revealing himself to his children? Has God been revealing himself to you? Do you know what he is like? Have you found out for yourself?

No guesswork! Give God a chance to tell you himself what he is like.

Interpretation

Never have I had a better time than when allowing the Holy Spirit to interpret Scripture to me. Always aware of such personal factors as maturity, need, and situation, the Holy Spirit will take Scripture and interpret them for you.

For example, do you find, as you read the Scriptures, that some parts make no sense to you at all? Do you just skip over them and go on?

Remember the verse about Moab? That's when I learned not to skip verses I could not understand. But now I ask the Holy Spirit for his interpretation.

Application

One of the most exciting things is hearing the Holy Spirit as he provides an application of Scripture for everyday living. When we meditate on the Scripture, we allow the Author to become our Explainer, our Interpreter, and the One who applies the truth to our lives.

Ephesians 5:25. Any Christian husband, myself among them, is often brought up short on reading Ephesians 5:25: "Husbands, love your wives, just as Christ loved the Church and gave Himself up for her."

We know that no man can actually do what the Scripture says: die for his wife on a cross, as Christ died for the church.

But it is the principle of loving one's wife with a deep sacrificial love that is applied to each of our situations by the Holy Spirit, who truly knows the needs of the spouse of each of us. He has given me such practical applications as:

"Take her out to supper tonight."

"Give her thirty minutes of undivided attention."

"Buy her a special gift."

"Wash the dishes for her tonight."

"Send her a card."

All of these are practical applications of one Scripture verse. They work — my wife is blessed, and so am I. When we fellowship with the Spirit, the Scriptures become alive. Relevant. Exciting. And practical on a day-by-day basis.

Philippians 4:13. Another example is from this well-known Scripture: "I can do all things through Him who strengthens me."

Taken at face value, this Scripture seems untrue. We cannot literally do *all* things through Christ who strengthens us. If you don't believe this, go outside and jump over the nearest building.

You can't, of course, so you will say to me, "That's not what it means." And I agree.

But the big question is, what *does* it mean? What does it mean for me right now? So many times the Holy Spirit has taken this great promise and applied it to a situation. . . .

After thirty-five years in the ministry, I forgot to go to a wedding that I was supposed to conduct for the daughter of a church member and personal friend.

I didn't really forget. I planned to go at 2:00 P.M., the usual time for weddings in our church. But this wedding was scheduled for 11:00 A.M.! I found out my error at noon, and I wanted to hide or run away.

In this situation, "I can do all things through Him who strengthens me" became: "You can go to the reception, Peter, and ask forgiveness."

My knees were like putty, but God assured me: "You have the strength *to go*, according to my promise in that verse, and the strength *to ask forgiveness*."

I went, and forgiveness was granted, but only because the Lord gave me strength. Philippians 4:13 became alive to me at 12:30 P.M. on Saturday, September 24, 1986.

There are many more applications of how the Holy Spirit applies Scripture to the "now" part of my life. Scripture is one of the easiest, best, safest, most blessed, and most profitable places to hear God speak to you.

How has he applied it to your life?

Lord Jesus, you are the key,
   the master key
      the master key to life.

You are the key that unlocks doors
   unlocks the door into the Father's presence
   unlocks the doors of opportunity
   unlocks the doors of relationships.

You are the key that locks doors
   You lock the doors of hell for me
   You lock the doors of death for me
   You lock the doors of protection for me.

Lord Jesus, you said
   "I give you the
      keys of the kingdom of heaven."

You gave us
   yourself.
You are the key to everything in the kingdom.
You are the key that locks up and unlocks.

Lord Jesus, with you
   we want to shut doors —
      and they open.
Lord Jesus, with you
   we want to open doors —
      and they shut.
Lord Jesus, with you
   we are safe.

Thank you
  for unlocking doors we cannot open.
Thank you
  for locking doors we cannot lock.
Thank you
  for being the key.

Thank You
  for giving us
    YOURSELF!

Peter M. Lord
Beholding Him

16

Hearing God in Prayer Life

Prayer is a two-way conversation between God the Father and one of us, his children. As such, it is one of the primary sources of fellowshiping with our Lord, if we but open our hearts to what he has to say. When we hear God in our times of meditation and prayer, there is much we learn about him and about ourselves.

Carole, a young staff member in our church, recently shared with me an experience she had while putting into practice what she had been learning about meditation. She had been out by the river early one morning, watching the sun rising above the mists on the water.

Overwhelmed by the beauty around her, Carole had praised the Lord by saying, "Jesus, your sunrise is so beautiful! I bet you really enjoy painting such a scene. In fact, I bet it's a real release for you after having to deal with us all day and all night. It must be your favorite part of the day."

Carole told me that God had answered her in the secret places of her heart: "Yes, Carole, I love sunrises and sunsets, and they are fun to paint, I love to paint them. But, rather than a release, it's just something I do on the side. My greatest joy is in you. You are much more important than any sunrise or sunset. In fact, I would leave a sunrise unfinished in a moment if you needed help and I were not big enough to do both. But I am big enough, so you need not worry. And even if I were not, you wouldn't need to worry, because you come first."

Do you think Carole could go out into a day discouraged after hearing this? No, she was excited, exhilarated, joyful in the Lord!

Have you ever wondered why most people pray for only five

minutes, repeat everything twice, and then feel like the prayer time lasted for thirty minutes?

Have you ever wondered why so few people spend any time in prayer at all?

Have you ever thought of the fact that most religious schools do not offer a course in prayer? Yet it was the *only* thing the disciples asked Jesus to teach them, and he did — by example and instruction.

The basic answer to all these questions is that when prayer is a one-way conversation, it is a very dull and boring experience. And that is exactly what prayer is to most people.

Do you talk very long on the telephone when you are not sure there is somebody on the other end? Of course not. You need to hear the other person's voice to have a meaningful conversation. So, too, is prayer transformed when it moves from a monologue to a dialogue — when you listen to God speak after you have spoken or when you listen to him speak before you utter a word.

Someone has jokingly said that God gave us two ears and one mouth so we could listen twice as much as we talked. When we learn to listen, prayer is vitalized. It is valuable in our lives, and it becomes very exciting.

Answered Prayers

God tells us how to pray so that he can answer that prayer. As my friend Adrian Rogers says, "All true prayer begins in heaven. God tells us what he wants us to ask so we can request it of him and he can do it. Our part is to agree with him and ask. Then we are to do whatever he says, even if he says to do nothing. That completes the circuit."

Let us see how all this works in a few practical illustrations from my own life. . . .

Trading Cars

Once, when Johnnie and I were in prayer, the Lord told us it was time to trade cars. (Yes, he is interested in every detail of life!)

Now, the God who made me knows how ignorant I am about the whole matter of cars. So in prayer he told me, "Ask Irby Moore [a friend and fellow Christian] to buy the car for you. Tell him how much you want to spend and basically what you want to use the car for."

I obeyed. The results were exciting:

1. When I talked to Irby, he told me he had recently looked for a car for himself and had his home computer full of information about all kinds of cars: advantages and disadvantages of makes and models and prices.
2. Irby agreed to help me, seeing it as an opportunity to minister in the Lord's name.
3. He found just exactly the right car for us.

God's way of getting us a car was such an exciting way! It was a way I had never thought of, would not have dreamed of, and had never done before. Nor has God led me to do it again.

My friend was blessed by being able to help me. I was blessed, for I dislike buying things I know little about. My family was blessed with just the right car.

Most importantly, I learned what a blessing it is to be able to communicate with my Father about all things and to take his advice. I want to do it more and more.

The Lost Wallet

While on a retreat a few years ago, I lost my wallet. This is how I entered it in my prayer journal: "Lord, I would like to have my wallet back. Is there any way that I can cooperate with you in finding it?"

His answer in my mind was: "No, Peter, you need do nothing except trust me. I will give your wallet back."

Although it was still lost, in my mind—through faith—I saw myself as having my wallet.

During the next few days, I would occasionally ask him about it. The answer would be the same. At one time I got impatient with God: "I want my wallet back *now*, Lord. There's that three-hundred-dollar check in it that someone gave me to get a new suit."

My impatience helped not one bit.

But six weeks later my wallet arrived through the mail 100 percent intact. Praise his name!

Praying for the Family

God also showed me how often we pray out of fear for our families. Then we tell God all he needs to do for them!

One morning when I was praying, the Lord said, "Stop. You are praying out of fear. In fact, today you do not need to ask me anything for your children. I will take care of them."

Another day as I was talking to the Lord about my daughter, Susan, he said, "Ask me to protect her today." So I did.

That day Susan was in an accident. Someone ran into the back of her Volkswagen, pushing it up into the car in front. Her car was totally demolished, but Susan was untouched.

On another occasion my wife was praying for our son Richard. He was on his way to California with a friend to go surfing. We were well aware he had shown no interest in spiritual matters, and Johnnie was telling the Lord all he needed to do to protect Richard.

"Johnnie," the Lord said, "if I do all you are asking me to do, I will not be able to do what I have planned to do. Commit Richard to me and do not pray out of your fear for his life."

Johnnie obeyed, but it was not easy to trust the Lord and keep on trusting, especially when Richard got into trouble in California. It never is easy to have faith when things seem to go from bad to worse.

But God had said, "I know the plans I have for you. Plans to prosper you and not to harm you, plans to give you a hope and a future." And God is always faithful to his promises.

Richard is now pastoring a church in Colorado. Not only that, but he also has a living, vital relationship with our Lord Jesus. We are able to fellowship and communicate with Richard about our Lord Jesus in many ways.

Our Lord has done exceedingly abundantly above all we can ask or even think. And he will continue to do so. When you allow prayer to be a time of fellowship with him, the One who loves you more than you are able to comprehend or understand will share his thoughts with you. Everyone who fellowships in prayer can recount experiences like the above, for they are regular occurrences for those who have learned to hear God in their prayer times.

Two Fundamental Requirements

There are two things that are as fundamental to our Christian journey as our two legs are to walking. If either of these basic ideas is damaged or crippled, so will be our Christian walk. Hearing God involves (1) a proper God-image, and (2) a proper self-image.

As we fellowship with the Lord, these two interrelated concepts are brought into his perspective. They are healed, changed, and matured. God loves to tell us what he is really like, so that we can have a proper God-image. And he loves to tell us what he thinks of us, so that we can have a proper self-image.

Nothing is more important than our relationship with God. What you think he thinks of you — what I think he thinks of me — is vital to fellowship and relationship with him. Like every father, lover, and true friend, God wants to tell us individually what he thinks of us. When we learn that God holds each of us in high esteem, we are transformed to reflect that image. Let us see how this works. . . .

Assessing Your Present Spiritual Self-Image

Self-image is an idea, the concept or picture of yourself that you hold in your mind. Your *spiritual* self-image is the idea of yourself that you hold about your relationship to God. It is what you think God thinks of you. And that, of course, depends on what you think God is like.

What do you think God thinks of you? If, right now, he was looking at you and describing you to the archangel Gabriel, what would he say? What names and adjectives would he use to describe you? Can you list six in the space below?

1.

2.

3.

4.

5.

6.

Maybe you would have to say, "I don't know what God thinks of me." If you would like to know, you can then find out through meditation.

But suppose you listed six words. And suppose the answers you gave there on the blank lines were incorrect. Do you realize that your errors would radically affect your attitude and behavior toward God?

In meditation you can find the truth — and, if necessary, change your mind. That's what repentance is — changing your mind to reflect what God says.

Arriving at a Correct Spiritual Self-Image

There are many possible ways to arrive at your spiritual self-image:

1. God tells you personally what he thinks of you, through the Scripture he brings to your mind and through his conversation with you. *This is the only reliable way.*
2. Other people — evangelists, pastors, friends — tell you what God thinks of you. This is inadequate because, at best, you are getting the information secondhand. Worse than that, they might be wrong!
3. The Evil One directly tells you what God thinks of you. But he is a deceiver!

The vast majority of Christians I have dealt with think too little of themselves — far less than God thinks of them. Some of them believe this is humility, but it is nothing more than inverted pride.

For every Christian who has an inflated self-image, there are twenty who think too lowly of themselves. *True humility is thinking about yourself the way God thinks about you.*

So, what does God think about you?

Try to personalize John 3:16 by replacing the words "the world" with your name.

God loved _____ so much that He gave His only begotten Son. God gave His Son so that _____ who believes in Him should not perish, but have eternal life.

There are many other Scripture passages that can be personalized in that way. But why don't you ask God directly what he thinks about you? He will be glad to tell you.

As I teach people to listen to God, I have them ask him such questions as: "Father, would you mind telling me what you think of me?" Or "Father, how much do you love me?"

To a woman in Ocala, Florida, God answered, "You are all the daughter I could ever want."

To a project manager at Cape Kennedy, the Lord said, "I think as much of you as of any other person."

When a young mother in our community asked, God replied, "You are worth more than you think. You are worth as much as I am."

Remember that anything's worth and value are determined by what a person is willing to pay for it. The Lord must have thought we are worth what he is, for he paid for us with his own life.

In meditation, as you fellowship with God, you will discover firsthand what God is really like and what he thinks of you. You will be in for some surprises — pleasant, uplifting, and encouraging good news. I have never seen any Christian discouraged at what he or she learns in this way, for this is Christ in fellowship with believers.

But *how can I know God's will?*

'ndeed,
>   there is hardly any question
>   that is more frequently asked than this.

Until we know God's voice
and how to hear Him speaking,
>   we are conscious of instability
>   in our Christian service.

In *multitudes of cases*
our *difficulty is*

NOT

unwillingness to go here, do this, or say that,

BUT UNCERTAINTY

as to whether God is telling us to act.[1]

1. Norman Grubb, *Touching the Invisible* (Fort Washington, Penn.: Christian Literature Crusade, 1940), p. 19.

17

Hearing God in Ministry

One afternoon, when I was making pastoral calls and had some unexpected extra time, I stopped my car and asked the Lord whom to visit. Very plainly, he gave me the picture in my mind of a man whose name I had forgotten. He also told me to call my wife, and she would give me his name and address.

I obeyed, got the name and address from Johnnie, and proceeded to the man's home. When I arrived, I was surprised to find an entire family waiting for me! They soon explained.

Earlier in the afternoon, they had called the church and asked the secretary if I could come by at a designated time. She had promised that I would but had not been able to contact me, since I did not return to the office that day.

There was no way for me to know about this person's need — except if the Lord Jesus guided me there.

You see, the man's heart was hungry for God. I felt like a modern-day version of Philip with the Ethiopian eunuch, for in ten minutes this man to whom I ministered had received the Lord Jesus into his life.

Exciting? Yes! The whole experience was. But especially important to me was this new evidence that the Lord and I could communicate so clearly and definitely. And I have had many other such experiences in my ministry. . . .

The Motel Story

One night at 10:30 P.M., we were in a Howard Johnson motel on I-4 in southern Georgia, on our way home from a Bible conference in North Carolina. As I lay on the bed preparing to go to sleep, the Lord Jesus said to me, "Get up and go to the motel office."

This was the last thing I wanted to do. Reluctantly and without emotion, I obeyed, thinking that God probably wanted me to witness to the young man at the desk.

As I approached the office, it was easy to see through the glass front that a man was checking in. I decided to wait outside until he left.

It was then I noticed that the traveler's car had a Florida tag from the same county as ours. When he came out in a minute or two, I introduced myself as Peter Lord, a pastor from Titusville.

The man gripped my shoulders with both hands and said, "You're the very person that I need to talk to. I am in great trouble," he went on. "As I drove up the highway, I called on God for help. Time and time again I was somehow restrained from stopping at a motel, which I had planned to do much earlier. When I got here, I felt a definite desire to stop, and so I drove in."

Great, isn't it? — to see how God works! This man cried for help. God heard him. God had me already in place, ready to help. He had seen me worshiping him and telling him how much I loved him and wanted to serve him. And so he told me to go to the office. He showed me someone in need.

"Dead Works" or Lasting Ministry?

Ministry is what God does through me for others. "Good works" are what I do at the command of God for others. They last for eternity. But "dead works" are what I do for others on my own, *supposedly* in the name of God. They do not last!

I have always been a hard worker. I have always put my heart into my ministry. But, after fifteen years as a pastor, I took a look back at what I had done in the Lord's service to determine the results of my work.

Much of it was in shambles. What had been built up had not really lasted. In fact, some of it was torn down. I looked at people who had worked in various churches and others who had made all kinds of decisions at the altar. And I saw that basically they remained unchanged. Or worse, they had reverted to worldly lifestyles.

This was devastating for me, for I was sincere and had worked very hard and had given up much of my life for my ministry

What had gone wrong?

Then I remembered reading something Watchman Nee had said: "God will only back and bless what He initiates." And I knew that in order for God to initiate, we have to hear God.

I realized that mine had been a ministry of dead works — dead because they had not begun with a word from God.

I had picked green fruit in order to get decisions and further my plans. I had placed or allowed people in positions of church leadership and responsibility who were totally unprepared. Some were not even managing their own homes wisely. I had built churches and organizations on the principles passed on to me by someone else who had used them successfully or by some agency whose business it was to promote "success."

Then God began to allow me to discover that all lasting ministry begins with a word from God. Then you walk with the Lord Jesus. You listen to the Holy Spirit and obey him. And you have an effective, exciting, enduring work.

God pointed me to his Son. For thirty years Jesus stayed in Nazareth. For thirty years he never taught, healed, delivered, or did much that you and I could recognize as "good works" — and yet the need was abounding.

Yet the Father said of Jesus at the River Jordan — *before* he had done any "good works" — "Thou art My beloved Son, in Thee I am well pleased" (Luke 3:22).

This is not our kind of evaluation. This is not our way of thinking. It is God's alone.

So how can you and I do "good works" in God's sight?

Jesus very simply outlines the secret of his ministry and gives us the secret for ours in the same breath. "Truly, truly I say to you, the Son can do nothing of Himself" (John 5:19a). How many times have I tried to do something alone, winging it! Yet Jesus tells us that even he can do nothing alone: ". . . for whatever the Father does, these things the Son also does in like manner" (v. 19b). With emphasis, he continues, "I can do nothing on My own initiative . . . but the Father abiding in Me does His works" (John 5:30a; 14:10b). He had been teaching. And healing. Having a one-on-one with Nicodemus and the Samaritan woman. Doing "good works." Yet what he is saying is:

> "... and My judgment is just, because I do not seek My own will, but the will of Him who sent me.... but the Father abiding in Me does His works" (John 5:30b; 14:10b).

Christ tells us that he was guided by an indwelling voice, not by an external appearance. God has sent the Holy Spirit to think his thoughts in us. The apostle Paul's statement that "we have the mind of Christ" (1 Cor. 2:16) is to be a reality in us as well.

In the words of Norman Grubb:

> We fail to bridge the gap within us between God's thoughts and God's word of faith because we are bound by the domination of the visible.
>
> We see the blind eye, the withered arm: Christ saw the will and power of His Father to heal, and spoke the word. "Stretch forth thine arm." "Receive thy sight."
>
> We see the five loaves and the multitudes, and say, "What are they among so many?" Christ saw His Father's invisible and unlimited supply, gave thanks for it, acted on the full assurance of it, and faith was seen to be "the giving of substance to things hoped for."[2]

I am not there yet. I do not always live by faith in my ministry, but I have discovered that this is the only way.

2. Ibid., p. 22.

> *The word of faith*
> IS NOT
> *some occasional*
> *rather exotic way*
> *of handling life's challenges,*
> BUT
> *the normal way of handling*
> *the most ordinary situations.*[1]

1. Norman P. Grubb, *Touching the Invisible* (Fort Washington, Penn.: Christian Literature Crusade, 1940), p. 19.

18

Hearing God for Life

If we open our hearts and minds to the Lord's guidance in all facets of our lives, we will discover that he is interested in everything about us. We can hear his voice and enter into fellowship with him, knowing that he cares about each of the day-to-day happenings that come our way. Learning that God communicates his continual concern for the ordinary things we care about is sometimes surprising, as it was to me in the following examples:

The "Toy" Calculator

In the summer of 1985, Johnnie and I made a tour of the Far East to speak to missionaries there. In Singapore I purchased a "toy" — a $2.50 calculator no bigger than a credit card. Its size and technology so fascinated me that I indulged in the luxury of an unnecessary purchase.

On the way home to Florida we stopped at Woodland Park, Colorado, to visit our son and his family. As a souvenir of the trip, I gave Richard the $2.50 calculator and began to show him how it worked. Except it didn't. All I got were sporadic numbers. My toy was broken!

I was disgusted. I had wasted money and had violated a concept I sought to live by: "The bitterness of poor quality lingers long after the sweetness of cheap price has been forgotten."

"Johnnie," I said to my wife, "don't ever let me buy a cheap thing like that again!"

Late that night I was still awake, trying to adjust to the ten-hour time change. As I fellowshiped with the Lord Jesus, he said, "Peter, there's nothing wrong with your calculator. It's just the mountains and the altitude here. Take it back to Florida and it will work properly."

Well, I did bring it back home with me and it's functioning as well as new. As always, Jesus knew what he was talking about.

The Blocked Toilet

Our son Richard has five sons of his own. One thing is inevitable — almost as certain as the sun coming up — if you have five small children, one of them will flush something large down a toilet.

Sure enough, one of the boys tried to flush away a wedge-shaped block. It stuck in the toilet trap. Richard tried and tried to get it out. Finally, thoroughly frustrated he called a plumber.

This paid professional worked at the problem with his tools for some time, but the block still stuck. Then he said, "The only way to get that out is with a sledge hammer."

"You mean I'll have to replace the toilet?" asked Richard.

"Yup," answered the plumber.

It was here that I arrived on the scene. Richard could not afford a new toilet and asked me to look at it. I worked fruitlessly a long time, and at last I gave up, too.

Then I asked the Lord for wisdom.

He told me exactly what to do. In ten minutes the block was out and the toilet was working again.

"Wait!" I can hear you say. "Our Lord is not interested in such mundane things as a $2.50 calculator and a jammed toilet!"

That's exactly what I used to think, till he reminded me, "My eye is on the sparrow — and it's on you, too. I am a father who cares about every aspect of my children's lives. I enjoy fixing things for you as you enjoy fixing things for your children."

Don't misunderstand me. God doesn't always say "Yes." He doesn't always give us an easy way out. I just want to point out that he cares, and he always answers in some way — if we will listen.

The Seat Belt

One Saturday in January 1986, I was headed to another town to make a ministry visit. As I left the house the Lord suddenly told me, "Fasten your safety belt." (This was before there was a mandatory seat belt law in Florida, and in those days I sometimes was careless about buckling up on short trips.)

My inner response was, "Oh, nothing is going to happen," but God said, "That's what everybody always thinks!" The message was clear, so I obeyed and fastened the belt this time.

Less than ten minutes later, I was driving along at fifty-five miles an hour on an open two-lane highway. Suddenly a car pulled out from a side road without stopping, zooming right into my path. There was no place to swerve safely, and I barely had time to hit the brakes.

A collision was unavoidable under the circumstances. Both cars were badly smashed. But I came out of it without even a bruise thanks to the Lord's watchcare, evidence that the Father cares and communicates at all times and in all things. Evidence of an active, vital fellowship with the Lord.

The Lost Diamond

While we were visiting our daughter in Texas, the diamond in my wife's engagement ring dropped out of its setting. It was only a small diamond — all I had been able to afford as a college student — but its sentimental value to both of us was great.

We asked the Lord to help us find it — and he did! It was a miracle, because it had fallen into the carpet pile, but God guided our search and we found the stone. Johnnie carefully put the diamond in a secure place in our suitcase, and one of the first things we wanted to do when we got home was to have it reset.

But when Johnnie unpacked at home and looked for the diamond, it wasn't where she had put it. She looked for it in every part of the suitcase but the diamond was gone. We searched intently and even called Texas and had our daughter look for it. Of course we prayed about it.

This time, there was no answer and no diamond. After a while we gave up. We accepted the loss as permanent. The diamond was forgotten, crowded from my mind by the immediacy of responsibilities.

One morning some time later, as I was fellowshiping with the Lord Jesus, he said to me, "Peter, the diamond is in your bedroom at home in the dresser."

And that's where it was! The tiny stone had gotten hidden in some seldom-used items in that suitcase and ended up in the dresser drawer! Now the diamond is again where it ought to be — on my wife's ring finger.

Some of the lessons I learned from these true stories and many others are:

1. God is interested in the smallest details of your life. "Toy" calculators, jammed toilets, and lost diamonds are equally valuable, even as "the very hairs of your head are all numbered" (Matt. 10:30, NIV).
2. God's answers are *often* delayed.
3. Many things happen when we are in fellowship with the Lord that do not happen if we are pressing him for answers. We must guard against our human tendency to use him and go to him only when we want something from him.

What Is Fellowship?

What does "fellowship" mean to you? Is it Kool-Aid and cookies with the Smiths after church on Sunday night? Is it a pot-luck supper on the church grounds? Or is it something more?

What does God have to say about his expectations for fellowship?

Jesus' beloved friend, John, says, "What we have seen and heard we proclaim to you also, that you also may have fellowship with us; and indeed our fellowship is with the Father, and with His Son Jesus Christ" (1 John 1:3).

What does God's kind of fellowship mean? What is fellowship from God's perspective?

People have fellowship because they have something in common. Because they are relatives or they have the same interest or are involved in the same activity. Because they feel the same emotion or have gone through similar experiences. This usually involves only one aspect of their lives: work, hobbies, church, or neighborhood association.

Fellowship with God differs from fellowship among people. Fellowship with him covers all of life. Nothing is left out. "God is faithful, through whom you were called into fellowship with His Son, Jesus Christ our Lord" (1 Cor. 1:9).

Fellowship with God is a lot like marriage. Two people marry because of love. They make a *commitment* to one another — a love covenant that encompasses all of life.

Out of this commitment, comes *communication* — the conversation that goes on between them. The conversation that sustains. That builds the relationship. That helps in working out the love covenant.

From this conversation come *goals and attitudes*. Then the husband and wife make *decisions* based on their fellowship with one another.

These decisions become *behavior and actions*, which are just a continuation and outworking of their fellowship. They include every area of life about which they are both concerned.

Fellowship with God the Father is simply the perfect shared life of a father with his dear child. It will cover every area of your life. It is your conversation and communion with each other. The Father who numbers every hair on his child's head, who sees each sparrow that falls, is surely interested in the calculators and toilets of his children!

The Bible also pictures Christ as the Bridegroom and the believer as his bride. God's kind of fellowship is the communication and communion between lovers as they anticipate living together forever. Our relationship with the Lord in the "forever" is a continuation of the relationship in the "now."

God is also the Comforter who lives in us to guide us into all truth. So fellowship is the communication between a Counselor and the counselee who comes to him, needing his advice.

To show you exactly what fellowship with God means in the life of an individual is the reason I shared with you the events of my own life in communing with him. God deals with each of us individually. These have been some of the ways he has dealt with me. There are others. I hope they will help you catch a glimpse of the wonder of it all and its overall effect on everything in your life.

My prayer is that you will desire to learn to hear him in an even deeper way.

At All Times — In All Things

I have purposely dealt separately with hearing God in the three areas that most people associate with the Christian life: Bible study, prayer, and ministry.

In this final chapter we come to a general area that I have found to be exciting, profitable, and specially blessed. That is God's desire to fellowship with us in all areas and matters of life, not just those we deem to be "religious," or spiritual. Norman Grubb writes:

> Communion with an indwelling Person is the privilege of all, and the unceasing experience of some.
> Guidance is the direct communication of the Spirit with our spirits and is not to be confused with the Scriptures.
> God's written word is the general guide to His people. The Bible is the inspired and infallible revelation of the principles of Christian living, and any individual guidance which does not conform to it is from a false source.
> The Spirit gives the guidance. It is always in conformity with the Scriptures, and may be in the words of Scripture, but it is the indwelling Spirit who guides.
> Romans 8:16 gives us the primary instance of spiritual communion in every believer's life: "The Spirit Himself bears witness with our spirit that we are children of God."
> *Guidance as to the details of living is only an extension of the inner speaking and hearing.*[2]

There are three basic things to remember as you fellowship with the Triune God:

1. God the Father is interested in all aspects of his children's lives.

2. Jesus the Bridegroom is interested in all aspects of the life of his bride-to-be, the body of believers.

3. The Holy Spirit as the indwelling Helper is there to help in all of life.

The more you learn to hear God, the more you will have the privilege of fellowship with him in the ordinary and mundane matters of life.

We cannot spend all of our time studying the Bible, or in concentrated prayer, or in ministry. But our Lord is just as interested in us at all other times and in all other matters. Both the little and the big.

One day when I was jogging and had a very heavy burden on my heart — one that I had not yet rolled over to God — I noticed a little dead sparrow on the side of the road.

2. Ibid., p. 22.

The Holy Spirit spoke to me so clearly: "Do you not know that the holy Father sees every little sparrow that falls? If he does that, don't you believe he is interested in every area of your life? Nothing is too small to bring to his attention. He cares about you. Bring all things to him — and then listen."

God is interested in the big things:

the college you attend

the car you need

the house you should or should not buy

the change of jobs

the rebellious teenager.

He is just as interested in the little things:

the blocked toilet

the discouraged wife

the parking space.

Hearing God *now* is a basic scriptural teaching. Hearing God is the privilege and right and responsibility of every born-again child of God.

I pray that this book has enticed you to see the reality and the benefits of hearing God not only through and in the Bible and prayer and Christian ministry, but in all of life.

You can have fellowship with God.

You can share your life with him.

When Christians pray, most realize that they are speaking to God. But many don't understand that God actually speaks back to them. And, since they don't expect Him to speak, they never learn to listen for Him.

I am so grateful to Peter Lord for this book, because he does such a masterful job of correcting this tragic misconception of God as a silent Father or a God we cannot hear.

I know I hear God as clearly as I hear my wife. He doesn't speak to me in an audible voice. He uses high-impact spiritual impressions, but the messages are as real and effective as audible words could be, and through them He gives me direction, correction and comfort.

There is really no room for debate as to whether God speaks to us. The biblical record clearly shows that God has spoken to His people since the beginning, when He walked with Adam and Eve in the Garden. He spoke to Moses, Abraham, Sarah, Isaac and Jacob and, of course, to all the prophets.

Referring to the Messiah's reign, Isaiah 30:21 prophesies that God will lead His people by His voice: "And your ears will hear a word behind you, 'This is the way, walk in it,' whenever you turn to the right or to the left."

In John 10:27, Jesus says, "My sheep *hear My voice*," and in John 16:13 He promises that the Holy Spirit will guide us by what "*He will speak*."

God didn't inspire the Bible to be written as only a love letter or an instruction manual but that we might also get to know Him personally. Hearing Him is a vital part of the intimate fellowship He desires with us. The ability to hear Him is so precious to me that I want everyone to understand and share it, and I am confident this book will help you make this present-day phenomenon a vital part of your walk with the Lord.

James Robison
LIFE Outreach International